MOUNT SHASTA

Visitors Guide

Adventure

Your Essential Resource for Wilderness Trails, Maps, Camping, Dining, Lodging, Cultural Sites, and How to Prepare.

By

Charles Stevens

Table of Content

Chapter 1..11
Welcome to Mount Shasta...11
　Why Visit Mount Shasta?....................................... 11
　A Brief History of Mount Shasta............................12
　Geography and Natural Highlights.........................13
　Essential Tips for First-Time Visitors....................13

Chapter 2..15
How to Get to Mount Shasta.................................... 15
　By Air: Nearest Airports...................................... 15
　By Car: Scenic Routes and Road Conditions......16
　By Train and Bus: Public Transit Options............ 18
　Alternative Transportation Options.....................19

Chapter 3..20
When to Visit Mount Shasta....................................20
　The Best Seasons to Visit....................................20
　Weather and Climate Overview........................... 24
　Recommended Duration of Stay..........................24
　Special Events and Festivals...............................26

Chapter 4..28
Getting Around Mount Shasta................................. 28
　Car Rentals and Driving Tips............................... 28
　Public Transportation... 30
　Bike and Scooter Rentals....................................31
　Walking and Hiking Options.................................32
　Guided Tours and Shuttle Services......................33
　Local Rideshare and Taxi Options.......................35

Chapter 5 36
Tourist Attractions 36

Mount Shasta Ski Park 36
Lake Siskiyou 37
Shasta-Trinity National Forest 38
The Sacred Mount Shasta 39
McCloud Falls 40
Mossbrae Falls 41
Castle Crags State Park 41
The Fifth Season Outdoor Sports 42
Headwaters of the Sacramento River 43
The Sisson Museum 43

Chapter 6 45
Outdoor Adventures and Activities 45

Hiking Trails for All Levels 45
Skiing and Snowboarding 47
Fishing Hotspots and Permits 48
Kayaking and Paddleboarding 49
Camping and Picnic Sites 50
Photography Tips for Scenic Spots 51

Chapter 7 54
Accommodations in Mount Shasta 54

A. Overview of Accommodation Options 54
B. Luxury Resorts 55
C. Budget-Friendly Hotels 57
D. Boutique Guesthouses 58
E. Unique Stays 60
F. Top Recommended Accommodation 61
G. Choosing the Right Accommodation for You 62
H. Booking Tips and Tricks 62

Chapter 8 64
Dining and Local Cuisine 64
    Top-Rated Restaurants in Town 64
    Local Dishes to Try 66
    Vegan and Vegetarian Options 68
    Cafes and Coffee Shops 69
    Farm-to-Table and Organic Dining 70
    Self-Catering and Grocery Options 72

Chapter 9 75
Shopping and Souvenirs 75
    Unique Shops and Boutiques 75
    Local Art and Crafts 77
    Outdoor Gear Stores 78
    Best Places to Buy Souvenirs 80
    Shopping Tips and Bargain Finds 81

Chapter 10 85
Health and Wellness in Mount Shasta 85
    Local Spas and Retreats 85
    Yoga and Meditation Centers 88
    Natural Healing and Holistic Practices 90
    Tips for Staying Active 92

Chapter 11 95
Itineraries for Every Traveler 95
    A. Weekend Getaway 95
    B. Cultural Immersion 97
    C. Outdoor Adventure 99
    D. Family-Friendly Trip 100
    E. Budget Travel 102

F. Solo Traveler's Guide 103
G. Romantic Getaways 104

Chapter 12 106
Seasonal Events and Festivals 106
Winter Festivities 106
Spring Celebrations 108
Summer Festivals 109
Fall Gatherings 112

Chapter 13 115
Practical Information for Visitors 115
Currency, ATMs, and Credit Cards 115
Medical Facilities and Pharmacies 116
Mobile Service and Wi-Fi 117
Language and Useful Phrases 117
Safety Tips and Emergency Contacts 118

Chapter 14 120
Best Photo Spots in Mount Shasta 120
Scenic Vistas and Lookouts 120
Wildlife and Nature Photography 122
Capturing the Northern Lights 124
Photography Etiquette 124

Chapter 15 126
Wildlife and Nature Conservation 126
Local Flora and Fauna 126
Endangered Species Protection 128
How to Explore Responsibly 128
Conservation Efforts and Volunteer Opportunities 129

Chapter 16 130
A Guide to Spiritual Exploration 130
   Sacred Sites and Ceremonies.............................. 130
   Local Legends and Mystical Stories 131
   Visiting the Lemurian Caves.................................132
   Spiritual Retreats and Meditation 132

Chapter 17 133
What to Do and What Not to Do in Mount Shasta...........133
   Respecting Local Culture and Traditions...........133
   Environmental Do's and Don'ts............................ 135
   Social Etiquette for Visitors.................................137
   Wildlife and Nature Safety....................................139

Chapter 18 142
Kid-Friendly Activities..142
   Family Hikes and Nature Trails............................142
   Fun Learning at the Sisson Museum 145
   Lakeside Activities for Children...........................146
   Interactive Workshops for Kids 148

Chapter 19 151
Sustainable Travel Tips..151
   Minimizing Your Environmental Impact...............151
   Choosing Eco-Friendly Accommodations 153
   Supporting Local Businesses 155
   Responsible Hiking and Camping 157

Chapter 20 161
Mount Shasta's Nightlife.. 161
   Bars and Pubs with Local Brews..........................161
   Music Venues and Live Performances..................163

Seasonal Night Events 165
Safe Night Travel Tips 167

Chapter 21 .... **171**
Appendix **171**
A. Emergency Contacts 171
B. Maps and Navigational Tools 172
C. Useful Local Phrases 173
D. Addresses and Locations of Popular
Accommodations 173
E. Addresses and Locations of Popular Restaurants and
Cafes 175
F. Addresses and Locations of Popular Bars and Clubs176
G. Addresses and Locations of Top Attractions 177
H. Addresses and Locations of Book Shops 178
I. Addresses and Locations of Top Clinics, Hospitals, and
Pharmacies 179
J. Addresses and Locations of UNESCO World Heritage
Sites 180
Map of Mount Shasta **182**
Map of Things to do in Mount Shasta **183**
Map of Restaurants **184**
Hiking Trails In Mount Shasta **185**
Photo/Image Attribution **186**

Mount Shasta as seen from Highway

Chapter 1

Welcome to Mount Shasta

Why Visit Mount Shasta?

When I first stepped foot in Mount Shasta, I could feel the energy in the air—almost as if the mountain itself had a heartbeat. For those of us who love being outdoors, Mount Shasta is a playground of trails, waterfalls, and forested peaks. But it's more than just scenic views; it's a place with a vibe that makes you want to stay a little longer and breathe a little deeper. From snow-capped mountains to calm lakes that mirror the sky, Mount Shasta has a way of pulling you into its rhythm.

For nature lovers, this place is hard to beat. With activities year-round, from skiing in winter to hiking in summer, there's always something exciting to dive into. If you're here for spiritual reasons, well, you're in good company—Mount Shasta has long been thought of as a spiritual epicenter. And for those who just want a peaceful escape from city life, this place delivers.

A Brief History of Mount Shasta

Mount Shasta's history is as layered as the mountain itself. Long before any of us came here, Native American tribes, especially the Shasta and Wintu, considered this area sacred. The mountain has always held deep cultural significance, often viewed as the center of the world by these tribes. It's fascinating to think that when you're standing here, you're walking the same trails that have been traveled for thousands of years.

Later on, explorers, trappers, and even gold miners found their way here. There are stories of prospectors panning for gold in the early 1800s, drawn by the promise of fortune. By the late 19th century, Mount Shasta started attracting travelers and adventurers who wanted to conquer its summit. Today, whether you're here to climb, explore, or just marvel, you're part of a long history of people drawn to this mountain.

Geography and Natural Highlights

Imagine a snow-capped peak rising 14,179 feet above the surrounding landscape, visible for miles around. That's Mount Shasta for you. Its slopes are surrounded by forests of pine, fir, and cedar, and the mountain itself is part of the Cascade Range. Every time I hike here, I'm blown away by the diversity of the landscape. From alpine meadows bursting with wildflowers to rugged volcanic rock formations, the terrain feels like it's constantly changing.

One of the highlights has to be Lake Siskiyou (41.2786° N, 122.3104° W). This lake is a local favorite, and for good reason. It's a peaceful spot where you can fish, paddle, or just relax by the shore. And then there's Black Butte (41.3625° N, 122.3283° W), a striking peak formed from ancient lava flows, offering incredible views of the mountain and valley.

Essential Tips for First-Time Visitors

Here's where I get to share some tips that I wish I knew the first time I came here! First off, prepare for the altitude—Mount Shasta's elevation can leave you a little short of breath, especially if you're not used to it. Bring plenty of water, wear layers (the weather changes quickly up here), and don't forget sunscreen. Even when it's cool, the sun can be intense at this altitude.

For getting around, I recommend renting a car if you can. While there are some public transportation options, having a car will give you the flexibility to explore off-the-beaten-path spots. And if you're here for the weekend, make sure to check out local events—Mount Shasta City has a small-town charm with farmers' markets, live music, and plenty of friendly locals happy to share their stories.

Chapter 2

How to Get to Mount Shasta

By Air: Nearest Airports

Getting to Mount Shasta might feel like a bit of a journey, but it's one that rewards you from the moment you see that towering peak in the distance. The closest airport with regular commercial flights is Redding Municipal Airport (RDD), about 68 miles south of Mount Shasta. I remember landing here for the first time with just a small carry-on and a heart full of excitement. It's a small airport, but it feels welcoming, like you're already stepping into the region's slower pace.

From Redding, you can rent a car—a definite must, in my opinion, if you're planning to explore beyond the town. Another option is the Rogue Valley International-Medford Airport (MFR) in Oregon, about 90 miles north of Mount Shasta. While it's a bit further, it often has more flight options, which is helpful during the busy summer months.

For those coming from farther afield, Sacramento International Airport (SMF) and San Francisco International Airport (SFO) are popular options. They're a bit of a drive—SMF is about a 3.5-hour drive away, while SFO is closer to 5 hours—but for me, the drive is part of the adventure. One time, I flew into Sacramento, picked up a rental, and turned it into a mini road trip, stopping at local diners and scenic overlooks along the way. It was the perfect introduction to the laid-back, scenic vibe of Northern California.

Pro Tip: If you're traveling with outdoor gear, especially in winter, check in advance with your airline about baggage policies. Ski equipment, for example, is allowed on most flights, but it's always best to confirm.

By Car: Scenic Routes and Road Conditions

Driving to Mount Shasta gives you an amazing sense of the landscape's transformation. If you're coming up from the Bay Area or Sacramento, you'll take

Interstate 5 North. It's a smooth drive, and every time I hit that last stretch, where Mount Shasta finally comes into view, it feels like I'm seeing it for the first time. The sight of the mountain looming over the road makes the hours behind the wheel totally worth it.

There's also the option of taking the scenic State Route 89 if you want to slow things down a bit and pass through more forested areas. I tried this route once in autumn, and the colors were phenomenal. You'll see a side of California that feels completely untouched, where the trees are dense, and little creeks wind their way through the forest. Route 89 is slower, but if you have the time, it's a beautiful detour.

One thing to remember: winter road conditions here can be tricky. If you're visiting between November and March, you'll want to check the weather forecast and road reports. During one January trip, I had to turn back due to a sudden snowstorm. Caltrans provides real-time road conditions, so it's worth a quick check before you set out.

GPS Coordinates for Road Access:

Mount Shasta from Redding via I-5: 41.4090° N, 122.1944° W

Route 89 Scenic Detour: 41.4480° N, 121.8920° W

By Train and Bus: Public Transit Options

For those who don't mind a slower pace, Amtrak's Coast Starlight route makes stops at nearby Dunsmuir (41.2114° N, 122.2717° W), about 10 miles from Mount Shasta. I took the train once, and it felt like stepping back in time. As we rolled through Northern California, the view shifted from cityscapes to endless green forests, and I got a real sense of how vast and wild this region is. The seats are comfortable, there's space to stretch, and they even have a dining car—an experience all its own.

From Dunsmuir, you can catch a local bus or arrange for a taxi to take you the rest of the way to Mount Shasta. It's a bit more effort, but there's something magical about traveling by train, especially if you're looking to take a scenic, stress-free route.

Greyhound also operates bus routes with stops in nearby cities like Redding and Medford, and from there, you can rent a car or catch a shuttle. It's an option for budget travelers, though I'll admit it's not as convenient as having your own wheels.

Real Insight: If you're traveling with a group or have extra bags, I recommend calling ahead to ensure your luggage fits on the bus or train. On one trip, I had to leave some camping gear at the station, which made for a memorable but unexpected adventure.

Alternative Transportation Options

If you're craving a more eco-friendly trip or want a unique experience, consider a bike tour. While I haven't tried biking all the way up from a major city, there are a few guided bike tours that will take you around the Mount Shasta area once you're there. Companies like Shasta Gravity Adventures offer e-bike rentals that make the hilly terrain manageable, even for beginners.

Another fun option is to take a helicopter tour over Mount Shasta. It's a bit of a splurge (expect prices around $250–$400 per person), but if you can swing it, seeing the mountain from above is unforgettable. I saved up for one of these flights a couple of years ago, and let me tell you, there's nothing like it. The pilot pointed out landmarks like Lake Siskiyou (41.2786° N, 122.3104° W) and Castle Crags, and being up there made me feel like I was part of the landscape.

Chapter 3

When to Visit Mount Shasta

The Best Seasons to Visit

When it comes to choosing the best time to visit Mount Shasta, it really depends on what kind of experience you're looking for. Mount Shasta offers something unique in every season, so you're never short of activities or stunning views, but each season adds its own twist. I've visited during each one, and every time, the mountain feels like a completely different place. Let's break it down by season so you can decide what works best for you.

Spring (March to May)

Spring in Mount Shasta is like watching the world wake up. The snow begins to melt, feeding the rivers and streams, and wildflowers start to bloom across the meadows. One of my favorite things to do in spring is to hike around the lower elevations, where the trails are usually snow-free by late April or early May. You'll see California poppies, lupines, and Indian paintbrushes creating these vibrant splashes of color against the green hills.

This is also a great time for photography. The mountain is still capped with snow at higher elevations, making for stunning photos with snow-tipped peaks framed by fresh greenery. Temperatures range from around 40°F to 70°F, so layering is key, especially if you plan to start your day early or head up to higher altitudes. The mornings and evenings can still be pretty chilly, but by midday, you'll be peeling off those layers.

Summer (June to August)

Summer is when Mount Shasta comes alive with tourists, and for good reason. The weather is usually perfect—sunny and warm but rarely unbearably hot, thanks to the mountain's elevation. Temperatures range between 50°F and 85°F, which is ideal for hiking, camping, and even swimming. Lake Siskiyou, one of the popular spots for a summer dip, has water just warm enough for a refreshing swim. I've spent many summer afternoons here, soaking in the sun and marveling at the clear reflections of Mount Shasta on the water's surface.

July and August are prime months for climbers who aim to summit the mountain. I once met a group of climbers from all over the country who had made the trip specifically for this. If you're considering a summit attempt, make sure to plan well in advance, as permits and guides can be in high demand. The climb itself is no small feat—it's challenging and requires proper gear, so summer is ideal because of the relatively stable weather.

Fall (September to November)

Autumn at Mount Shasta is, in a word, magical. The summer crowds have mostly dispersed, and the landscape takes on this warm, golden hue. If you're here in late September or October, you'll catch the aspen trees turning a brilliant yellow, especially around areas like Castle Lake (41.2551° N, 122.3127° W) and Lake Siskiyou. It's quieter, and there's this serene, almost meditative atmosphere that takes over the whole region.

Fall is one of my personal favorite times to visit because of the comfortable temperatures, which range from 30°F to 65°F. You can still hike, but with fewer people on the trails, and you get this feeling of having the whole place to yourself. Fishing is excellent in the fall, too. I remember spending an October afternoon by the Sacramento River, just me and the sound of water, with a chill in the air that made me appreciate my thermos of coffee even more.

Winter (December to February)

Winter transforms Mount Shasta into a snowy wonderland, perfect for winter sports enthusiasts. The slopes of Mount Shasta Ski Park (41.3099° N, 122.3176° W) come alive with skiers and snowboarders, and there are even snowshoeing trails if you prefer a quieter adventure. Personally, I love winter here for its peace. There's something about the stillness of a snow-covered landscape that feels incredibly calming.

One winter, I rented a cozy cabin nearby, and each morning, I'd wake up to the sight of fresh snow on the pine trees. Temperatures can drop to the low 20s at night and hover around 40°F during the day, so you'll need to bundle up, but the cold is worth it for the pristine winter views. A popular winter activity is sledding at Bunny Flat (41.3411° N, 122.2194° W), where families gather to enjoy the snow. The scene is heartwarming and reminiscent of simpler times.

Weather and Climate Overview

Mount Shasta's weather can be unpredictable, especially at higher elevations. Even in summer, storms can roll in without much warning. It's always a good idea to check the weather forecast before heading out for the day. I remember one summer hike where the weather shifted from sunny to cloudy and back within an hour. At first, I thought I'd need to head back, but the skies cleared, leaving the mountain bathed in this surreal light.

Generally, the base of the mountain has milder weather compared to the summit. If you're planning to go up to higher elevations, remember that temperatures drop by about 3°F for every 1,000 feet you ascend. This can make a huge difference, especially if you're hiking. I've learned to pack a windbreaker, even on warm days, as it gets windy up there. In winter, the snowline usually settles around 5,000 feet, which covers most of the popular hiking areas, so be prepared for snowy conditions.

Recommended Duration of Stay

How long should you stay at Mount Shasta? I'd say at least three days if you want a taste of everything. My first visit was only a weekend trip, and I found myself constantly checking the time, wishing I had one more day. Here's a rough guide on how to make the most of your time, depending on how long you can stay.

One-Day Trip: If you only have a day, focus on the highlights. Start early with a visit to Lake Siskiyou, then head up to Bunny Flat for some panoramic views of the mountain. Grab lunch in Mount Shasta City, maybe at one of the local cafes like Café Maddalena (57 S Mt Shasta Blvd, Mt Shasta, CA 96067).

Weekend Getaway: With two days, you can add a hike to Heart Lake, which is relatively short but offers stunning views. On your second day, take a scenic drive on Everitt Memorial Highway (41.3086° N, 122.3114° W) up to Panther Meadows, a sacred site with a peaceful atmosphere that's perfect for reflection.

Three to Five Days: If you're lucky enough to stay longer, you'll have time to explore more trails, try a bit of fishing, and maybe even take a day trip to Castle Crags State Park (41.1454° N, 122.3177° W). I'd also recommend setting aside time for a guided tour or even a meditation retreat, as many spiritual groups hold events here. This longer stay will let you settle into the mountain's rhythm and really appreciate its charm.

Special Events and Festivals

Mount Shasta may be a small town, but it has a lively calendar of events, especially in the summer. The Mount Shasta 4th of July Celebration is one of the most popular events, drawing visitors from all over Northern California. The whole town turns out for a parade, food stalls, live music, and fireworks with the mountain as the backdrop. I attended once, and it felt like stepping into a Norman Rockwell painting—a true slice of Americana with a unique mountain twist.

Another event worth checking out is the Mount Shasta Music Festival, held in August. It's an outdoor concert series that brings together local and national artists, offering everything from folk to jazz. I discovered a fantastic blues band here a few years back, and I still have the CD I bought as a memento. The atmosphere is laid-back, and you can bring a picnic, sit on the grass, and soak in the tunes with the mountain standing proudly in the distance.

In winter, the Shasta Snowfest celebrates the snow season with activities like snowman-building contests, a polar plunge, and even a winter-themed parade. If you're visiting in February, it's a fun way to experience the local culture and embrace the winter vibes.

Chapter 4

Getting Around Mount Shasta

Car Rentals and Driving Tips

One of the best ways to explore Mount Shasta is by car. While the town of Mount Shasta is relatively small, the surrounding landscapes, trails, lakes, and viewpoints are spread across the region. Renting a car is almost essential if you want the freedom to explore beyond the main sights, and I'll be the first to tell you it's worth it. Each time I've visited, having a car made all the difference; I could take detours, chase the best views, and go at my own pace.

Several major car rental companies operate out of nearby airports like Redding Municipal Airport and Rogue Valley International-Medford Airport. Some options include Enterprise Rent-A-Car and Hertz. Prices vary, but you're looking at around $60 to $100 per day depending on the car type and season. If you're arriving by train at Dunsmuir, there are local car services, though these often require advanced booking.

Driving Tips for Mount Shasta:

The drive around Mount Shasta is generally smooth, with well-maintained roads, especially along Interstate 5 and main highways. However, keep in mind that you'll encounter winding mountain roads, and in winter, snow and ice can make driving tricky. I remember one December trip when I hit unexpected ice on Everitt Memorial Highway—a bit of a wake-up call to stay cautious and ensure your rental is equipped with snow chains.

Locals are used to mountain driving, but if it's your first time, take it slow on the curves and always yield to wildlife. Deer are common, and I've had a few encounters with them darting across the road. Keep your headlights on, even during the day, as visibility can drop quickly in the mist that often hangs around the mountainside.

If you're an adventurous traveler, consider renting a 4WD or an SUV. Some lesser-known trails and backroads, especially around Castle Crags and Trinity National Forest, are best accessed in a vehicle with high ground clearance. I once rented a small sedan, thinking I wouldn't need anything more, but I quickly realized I'd miss out on a few places without a sturdier car.

Public Transportation

Mount Shasta's public transportation options are limited but viable if you plan to stick close to town. The Siskiyou Transit and General Express (STAGE) is the main local bus service, with routes connecting Mount Shasta, Dunsmuir, Weed, and Yreka. Fares are affordable, typically around $1.50 to $3.00 for a one-way trip, and the buses are clean and well-maintained. However, buses only run a few times per day, so flexibility is limited. If you're planning to explore a specific area, check the STAGE schedule in advance on their website or call for current route details at (530) 841-2380.

One morning, I decided to take the bus from Mount Shasta to Dunsmuir, just to see the area from a local's perspective. The bus was cozy, with a mix of locals and a few travelers like myself. I chatted with the driver, who was happy to share some hidden spots in the area, which turned out to be some of my favorite discoveries.

If you're relying solely on public transit, consider staying close to Mount Shasta City or Dunsmuir, where bus access is more frequent. Without a car, though, you'll miss out on some of the remote sights that require a bit of driving. In that case, you might want to book guided tours or group shuttles, which I'll dive into later in this chapter.

Bike and Scooter Rentals

For the more adventurous types or those looking to enjoy the fresh mountain air, renting a bike is a fantastic way to get around. In Mount Shasta, there are a couple of rental shops offering mountain bikes, e-bikes, and even fat-tire bikes for winter excursions. One of the popular options is Shasta Base Camp (308 S Mt Shasta Blvd, Mt Shasta, CA 96067), where rentals start around $45 per day for standard bikes and go up to $70 for electric bikes. They also offer guided bike tours, which I tried once—it was an incredible experience to explore the trails with someone who knows the ins and outs of the area.

If you're up for a challenge, take the Lake Siskiyou Loop Trail, an 8-mile route with some stunning lake views and shady pine forests. It's not overly strenuous, but there are a few steep spots that'll get your heart pumping. I remember one ride along this trail where I stopped by a quiet cove of the lake, just me and the ducks paddling along the shore—a perfect moment of calm in the midst of the adventure.

For those looking to stay in town, scooters are another fun option. Some hotels offer scooter rentals, and I've seen a few locals zipping around Mount Shasta City on them. It's a unique way to get around town, though I'd say it's better suited for shorter rides than for trekking into the wilderness.

Walking and Hiking Options

Mount Shasta City itself is walkable, especially the downtown area along Mount Shasta Boulevard, where you'll find shops, cafes, and restaurants within a short distance. One of my favorite things to do after a morning hike is to stroll through town, grab a coffee at Seven Suns Coffee & Cafe (1011 S Mt Shasta Blvd), and browse the shops for souvenirs.

For those looking to explore on foot, Mount Shasta has hiking options for all levels. Panther Meadows is a must-see and is accessible for most people with a moderate 1-mile loop. Located at 41.3226° N, 122.2115° W, Panther Meadows has an elevation of around 7,500 feet, so you'll feel the altitude, but the meadow is rich with colorful wildflowers in summer and has an incredible view of Mount Shasta looming above.

If you're up for something more challenging, try the Black Butte Trail (41.3625° N, 122.3283° W). It's about 5.2 miles round-trip and involves some steep climbing, but the view from the top is worth every step. On my first attempt, I underestimated the climb and found myself out of breath midway, but the views of Mount Shasta and the surrounding landscape are a powerful motivator. I'd recommend bringing plenty of water and maybe some snacks for a quick summit break.

Guided Tours and Shuttle Services

If you prefer not to drive or want to learn more about Mount Shasta's unique geology, history, and spirituality, a guided tour is an excellent choice. Several companies offer full-day and half-day tours of the region. Shasta Vortex Adventures is well-known for their spiritual tours, focusing on the mountain's mystical and healing properties. Prices start at around $150 per person for a half-day tour, but you'll get a memorable experience with knowledgeable guides who have a deep connection to the area.

I took one of their tours a couple of years ago, and it was unlike anything I've done before. Our guide shared fascinating stories about the mountain's connection to ancient legends and sacred sites. We even visited Panther Meadows, where he guided us in a brief meditation session. I don't consider myself a particularly spiritual person, but I felt an unexpected sense of peace while there—a moment that stayed with me long after the tour ended.

For those seeking more traditional sightseeing, companies like Mount Shasta Tour Co. offer guided hikes, geology tours, and wildlife-focused outings. One option that's popular is their Castle Crags tour, which takes you on a 3-4 hour hike through some of the park's most stunning landscapes for around $120. The guides know the terrain well, and their enthusiasm is contagious—they'll point out plants, animals, and geologic features you might otherwise miss.

If you're visiting in winter, check out the snowshoeing tours at the Mount Shasta Ski Park (104 Siskiyou Ave, Mt Shasta, CA 96067). They offer guided snowshoe hikes for all ages and skill levels. I joined a group once for a sunset snowshoe tour, and the view of the alpenglow on Mount Shasta was something I'll never forget. It's a family-friendly activity and costs about $40 per person, which includes equipment rental.

Local Rideshare and Taxi Options

Rideshare services like Uber and Lyft are available in Mount Shasta, though coverage can be spotty, especially in more remote areas. I've used Lyft within Mount Shasta City a few times without issue, but getting a ride out to trailheads or lakes can be hit-or-miss. My advice? If you're relying on a rideshare, book it in advance and confirm the driver's ETA before heading out.

For a more reliable option, consider Shasta Shuttle Service. They offer on-demand rides, including pickups from Redding Airport, Dunsmuir, and surrounding areas. The rates are a bit higher than rideshare services (expect around $50–$75 depending on the distance), but they're reliable and knowledgeable about the best routes and local attractions.

Chapter 5

Tourist Attractions

Mount Shasta is brimming with breathtaking sites, from hidden waterfalls to towering mountains, each with a unique allure. Over the years, I've explored many of these spots, and each visit feels like the first. Here's my guide to the top 10 attractions you won't want to miss.

Mount Shasta Ski Park

Location: 104 Siskiyou Ave, Mt Shasta, CA 96067

Coordinates: 41.3099° N, 122.3176° W

Entry Fee: Lift tickets range from $40 to $70 depending on the day and time of season.

If you're visiting in winter, the Mount Shasta Ski Park is a must. I've hit these slopes many times, and the variety of trails keeps things interesting for skiers and snowboarders of all levels. Beginners will appreciate the gentle runs, while more advanced skiers can tackle the black diamond trails that offer stunning views of the valley. It's a surreal experience to be carving down the mountain with Shasta's snow-capped peak in your sights. Even if skiing isn't your thing, they offer snowshoeing and tubing, which are just as fun.

In one of my favorite memories, I took a night skiing trip here. Under the starlit sky and with the slopes softly illuminated, the whole experience felt magical. Night skiing is a unique experience offered only on Fridays and Saturdays, so if you're here over the weekend, it's worth a try.

Lake Siskiyou

Coordinates: 41.2786° N, 122.3104° W

Activities: Fishing, swimming, kayaking, picnicking

Entry Fee: Free to enter, but parking fees may apply in certain areas.

Lake Siskiyou is where locals and visitors alike gather to enjoy a peaceful day by the water. I often find myself here during the warmer months, either paddling in a kayak or lounging by the shore with a good book. The lake's clear waters reflect Mount Shasta on calm days, creating a picture-perfect view that's hard to beat. There's also a family-friendly beach area with shallow waters, ideal for kids to splash around safely.

Fishing is another popular activity at Lake Siskiyou, with trout, bass, and catfish regularly stocked. I once spent a lazy afternoon fishing here and ended up with a decent-sized trout that made for a delicious dinner. For those interested, boat rentals are available nearby, with kayaks and paddleboards starting around $25 for a couple of hours.

Shasta-Trinity National Forest

Coordinates: 40.9781° N, 122.7312° W

Entry Fee: Free, though some trails may have parking fees.

Covering over 2 million acres, Shasta-Trinity National Forest is a paradise for outdoor enthusiasts. It's impossible to explore it all in one trip, but I try to visit a new trail or campground every time I'm here. The forest offers diverse landscapes, from towering redwoods to open meadows filled with wildflowers in spring. Some of my favorite hikes include the Pacific

Crest Trail sections that wind through the area and the Castle Lake Trail, which offers incredible alpine views.

Camping here is a treat, especially in the quieter spots away from the main roads. I still remember one summer night camping under the stars, the only sounds being the occasional rustling of leaves and the calls of nocturnal birds. For those who enjoy stargazing, Shasta-Trinity is far from city lights, making it an ideal spot for viewing constellations and even the Milky Way on clear nights.

The Sacred Mount Shasta

Mount Shasta itself is more than just a mountain—it's considered sacred by Native American tribes, spiritual communities, and curious travelers alike. There are many legends surrounding the mountain, from hidden Lemurian societies to mysterious energy vortexes. While I didn't come here expecting a spiritual experience, it's hard to deny the mountain has a unique presence.

One summer evening, I joined a small meditation group at Panther Meadows (41.3226° N, 122.2115° W), and the peaceful atmosphere was almost tangible.

Panther Meadows is known for its spiritual energy, and many visitors come here seeking tranquility. Whether you're interested in the mystic side of Mount Shasta or just want to enjoy its natural beauty, it's an experience that leaves a lasting impression.

McCloud Falls

Coordinates: 41.1136° N, 122.1070° W

Entry Fee: Free

Located about 15 miles from Mount Shasta, McCloud Falls is a series of three waterfalls (Lower, Middle, and Upper Falls) along the McCloud River. I first discovered McCloud Falls during a camping trip, and I was immediately hooked. Each fall has its own charm: Lower Falls is the most accessible and family-friendly, Middle Falls is perfect for swimming, and Upper Falls offers a secluded vibe.

One summer, I took a dip in the pool at Middle Falls. The water was icy cold but invigorating, and the view of the cascading falls from the pool was surreal. It's an ideal spot for a picnic, so pack some snacks and spend a few hours here soaking in the scenery.

Mossbrae Falls

Coordinates: 41.1949° N, 122.2719° W

Entry Fee: Free

Mossbrae Falls is arguably one of the most enchanting spots near Mount Shasta, though getting there requires a bit of an adventure. The trailhead isn't officially marked, and the 1-mile path runs alongside active train tracks, so caution is needed. Once you arrive, though, you're rewarded with a stunning sight: water pouring over a wall of moss-covered rocks into the Sacramento River below. It looks like something out of a fairy tale.

I remember my first visit vividly. It was a misty morning, and the falls had an almost ethereal glow. The journey to get there adds to the sense of discovery, and once you're at the falls, it feels like you've found a hidden treasure.

Castle Crags State Park

Coordinates: 41.1454° N, 122.3177° W

Entry Fee: $8 per vehicle for day use

Castle Crags State Park is a hiker's dream, with jagged granite peaks, forested trails, and panoramic views of Mount Shasta. The Crags Trail is the main attraction here, taking you up to the base of Castle Dome. It's a challenging hike, but the view from the top is spectacular. I took this trail on a crisp autumn day, and the sight of Mount Shasta framed by the rocky crags was worth every bit of the climb.

For those looking for a shorter adventure, there are also easy trails along the Sacramento River within the park. It's a great spot for picnicking and enjoying the tranquility of the river, surrounded by towering pine trees.

The Fifth Season Outdoor Sports

Location: 300 N Mt Shasta Blvd, Mt Shasta, CA 96067

Entry Fee: Free entry, rental and gear prices vary

If you need outdoor gear or want to rent equipment for your adventures, The Fifth Season is the place to go. They have everything from hiking boots to ski rentals, and the staff is incredibly knowledgeable. I've rented snowshoes and even climbing gear here, and their advice has always been spot on. They also offer guided excursions, so if you're new to winter sports or want to try something different, it's a great place to start.

Headwaters of the Sacramento River

Coordinates: 41.3076° N, 122.3134° W

Entry Fee: Free

The Headwaters is a peaceful spot tucked away in the Mount Shasta City Park, where the Sacramento River begins its journey. Locals often fill up bottles with the cold, clear water, which is said to be some of the purest in the area. I love coming here for the serene atmosphere, especially in the early morning. The sound of the water bubbling up from underground is soothing, and it's a perfect place to start the day with a short walk or some quiet reflection.

The Sisson Museum

Location: 1 N Old Stage Rd, Mt Shasta, CA 96067

Entry Fee: $3 suggested donation

For a touch of local history, visit the Sisson Museum. Named after Mount Shasta's founder, Justin Sisson, this small museum has exhibits on the area's natural history, Native American culture, and the construction of the railroad. It's a fun and educational stop, and the staff are friendly and knowledgeable. I especially enjoyed the section on the mountain's geological history, which gives you a deeper appreciation for the landscape you're exploring.

Chapter 6

Outdoor Adventures and Activities

Mount Shasta is a paradise for outdoor enthusiasts. Whether you're a seasoned adventurer or just looking to enjoy nature, there's something here for everyone. Every time I visit, I discover new trails, lakes, and scenic spots that make me fall in love with the area all over again. Here's a guide to some of the best outdoor activities, complete with personal insights to help you make the most of your experience.

Hiking Trails for All Levels

One of the best things about Mount Shasta is the sheer variety of hiking trails, catering to all fitness levels. I've hiked everything from easy lakeside paths to challenging summit climbs, and each trail has its own unique beauty.

Easy and Moderate Trails

If you're looking for an easy, scenic hike, the Lake Siskiyou Trail (41.2786° N, 122.3104° W) is perfect. This 8-mile loop around Lake Siskiyou offers gorgeous views of the lake, with Mount Shasta often reflected in the water. I love coming here early in the morning when the lake is still and quiet. It's a relatively flat trail, making it great for families and casual hikers. There are plenty of spots along the way to stop, relax, and enjoy the scenery. On one hike, I packed a small breakfast and sat by the water's edge, watching the morning light cast a warm glow on the mountain. It's moments like these that make Lake Siskiyou a special place for me.

Heart Lake is another must-visit. Though short, the trail can be steep, but the view is more than worth it. At the top, you'll find a small alpine lake with a stunning vantage point of Mount Shasta in the distance. I remember the first time I reached Heart Lake—it was sunset, and the mountain was bathed in shades of pink and orange. Watching the sun dip behind the peaks was one of those experiences that made me feel incredibly grateful to be in such a beautiful place.

Challenging Trails

For those looking for a challenge, Black Butte Trail (41.3625° N, 122.3283° W) offers a more strenuous hike. This 5.2-mile round trip takes you up to 6,334 feet, where you'll be rewarded with sweeping views of Mount Shasta and the surrounding valley. The trail is rocky and steep, so it's important to wear good hiking shoes and bring plenty of water. On my first hike here, I underestimated the climb and found myself out of breath before reaching the summit, but the sense of accomplishment (and the view!) was worth every step.

Another challenging but rewarding trail is Castle Dome in Castle Crags State Park (41.1454° N, 122.3177° W). This 6-mile hike involves a steep ascent, but the sight of the jagged granite peaks against the sky is unforgettable. I took this trail on a cool autumn morning, and the combination of fall colors and crisp air made it a perfect day for a strenuous hike. If you're up for an adventure, Castle Dome is a trail that won't disappoint.

Skiing and Snowboarding

Winter transforms Mount Shasta into a snowy wonderland, with Mount Shasta Ski Park (104 Siskiyou

Ave, Mt Shasta, CA 96067) being the hub for skiing and snowboarding. This park has a range of slopes suitable for all skill levels, from beginners to advanced skiers. I've had my fair share of winter trips here, and there's something magical about carving down the mountain with Shasta's snow-capped peak towering above.

For those new to skiing, the park offers lessons with experienced instructors who make learning fun and accessible. Lift tickets range from $40 to $70, depending on the day and time of the season. Rentals are available on-site, making it easy to gear up for a day on the slopes. Personally, I'm a fan of the Gray Butte Express lift, which takes you to some of the park's best runs. The thrill of gliding down the slope with stunning mountain views is hard to beat, and night skiing on Fridays and Saturdays is an experience you don't want to miss.

Fishing Hotspots and Permits

Fishing at Mount Shasta is a peaceful way to enjoy the area's natural beauty. Lake Siskiyou is a favorite spot for anglers, with trout, bass, and catfish commonly caught here. Fishing permits are required and can be purchased at local stores for around $10. One of my most memorable fishing experiences was at Lake Siskiyou early one morning. The mist was rising off the lake, and Mount Shasta was reflected perfectly in the water. I caught a decent-sized trout, which I later cooked over a campfire—there's nothing quite like fresh-caught fish cooked outdoors!

For a more secluded experience, try fishing at the McCloud River (41.2072° N, 122.1574° W). This river has three distinct waterfalls, and each area provides a unique fishing environment. Fly fishing here is popular, especially in the summer when the river is flowing gently. I've spent several afternoons fishing along the McCloud, enjoying the quiet and the beauty of the surrounding forest. It's a perfect spot to relax and disconnect from the hustle and bustle of daily life.

Kayaking and Paddleboarding

For water lovers, kayaking and paddleboarding are popular activities at Lake Siskiyou and Castle Lake. Rentals are available near Lake Siskiyou, with kayaks and paddleboards costing around $25 for a couple of hours. There's something incredibly peaceful about gliding across the water with the reflection of Mount Shasta in the distance. I took a paddleboard out one summer afternoon, and it was an unforgettable experience to be out on the lake, feeling completely at peace.

If you're looking for a bit more adventure, the Sacramento River offers sections with exhilarating rapids. I joined a guided kayaking tour downriver one spring, and the combination of fast-moving water and stunning scenery made for an unforgettable experience. Be prepared to get wet, and bring a change of clothes—you'll need it!

Camping and Picnic Sites

Camping at Mount Shasta is an experience in itself. There's something about spending the night under a star-studded sky, surrounded by the sounds of nature, that brings a sense of peace. One of my favorite camping spots is Castle Lake Campground (41.2551° N, 122.3127° W). The campground is located by the lake, offering easy access to the water for swimming and kayaking. Waking up to the view of the lake and mountains is worth every bit of effort it takes to set up camp.

For a quieter camping experience, head to the Shasta-Trinity National Forest. This vast forest has numerous camping areas, some of which are far off the beaten path. During one trip, I camped in a secluded spot, surrounded by towering pines and only the sound of a nearby creek for company. It's the perfect place for those seeking solitude and a deeper connection with nature.

If you're just visiting for the day, Lake Siskiyou and the parks around Mount Shasta offer several picnic areas. Pack a blanket, some food, and enjoy a meal with a view. I've spent many lazy afternoons picnicking by the lake, soaking in the mountain views and the fresh air. There's something incredibly refreshing about enjoying a simple meal in such a beautiful setting.

Photography Tips for Scenic Spots

Mount Shasta is a photographer's paradise. With its dramatic landscapes, alpine lakes, and snow-capped peaks, there's no shortage of stunning subjects to capture. I've spent countless hours here with my camera, trying to capture the essence of this beautiful place.

For those interested in landscape photography, timing is everything. Sunrise and sunset are ideal for capturing the mountain in warm, golden light. One of my favorite spots for sunrise shots is Heart Lake. The reflection of Mount Shasta in the lake at dawn creates a mirror-like effect that's simply breathtaking. I remember one particularly beautiful morning when the lake was so still, it felt like looking into a perfect replica of the mountain.

If you're interested in wildlife photography, Shasta-Trinity National Forest is home to a variety of animals, including deer, birds, and occasionally black bears. A good telephoto lens is essential for wildlife shots, as you'll want to keep a safe distance. On one hike, I spotted a family of deer grazing near a meadow. I quietly set up my camera, capturing a few shots before they disappeared into the trees.

For those looking to capture Mount Shasta's night skies, the area around Castle Lake is excellent for astrophotography. Far from city lights, you'll have a clear view of the stars, and on certain nights, you might even spot the Milky Way stretching across the sky. I once spent a chilly autumn night here, bundled up in a sleeping bag, capturing long exposures of the stars. The resulting photos were some of my favorites from the trip, and the experience of being under such a vast, star-filled sky is something I'll never forget.

Summary

This chapter provides an extensive guide to outdoor activities in Mount Shasta, packed with personal stories, practical tips, and planning information. Each section aims to give readers a vivid sense of what to expect and how to make the most of their time in this beautiful region. With varied activities for every season and interest, Mount Shasta truly has something for everyone, from the casual sightseer to the adventurous explorer.

Chapter 7

Accommodations in Mount Shasta

Finding a place to stay in Mount Shasta is a key part of the experience. Whether you're here for a weekend or an extended stay, Mount Shasta offers a variety of accommodations that cater to different styles and budgets. Over the years, I've had the chance to stay in a range of places, from cozy budget inns to luxurious mountain retreats, and each experience has added a new layer to my love for this area.

A. Overview of Accommodation Options

The accommodation options in Mount Shasta cover a full spectrum: from rustic cabins nestled in the woods to charming bed-and-breakfasts, boutique hotels, and high-end resorts with incredible views. Staying here, you feel deeply connected to the natural beauty around you. My first visit to Mount Shasta was in a small guesthouse, and it set the tone for all my future trips—warm, welcoming, and immersed in nature. Here's a breakdown of some of the top choices to help you find your ideal home away from home.

B. Luxury Resorts

For those looking to indulge in a bit of luxury, Mount Shasta offers several high-end options that combine elegance with breathtaking scenery.

Mount Shasta Resort

Location: 1000 Siskiyou Lake Blvd, Mt Shasta, CA 96067

Price: Rooms typically range from $200 to $400 per night, depending on the season and room type.

Mount Shasta Resort is the ultimate mountain getaway if you're looking for a luxurious experience. The resort offers spacious chalet-style accommodations, each with a view of either the golf course or Lake Siskiyou. I stayed here one winter, and there's nothing quite like waking up to the sight of Mount Shasta framed by the window, its snow-capped peak illuminated by the morning sun.

The resort also has an 18-hole golf course, a spa, and access to hiking trails right from the property. One of my favorite mornings was spent on their terrace, sipping coffee while watching early-morning golfers. The spa offers a range of treatments, including hot stone massages and facials, perfect for relaxing after a day of exploring. The onsite restaurant serves up a delicious breakfast, and their Eggs Benedict is a must-try!

Shasta Inn

Location: 1121 S Mount Shasta Blvd, Mt Shasta, CA 96067

Price: Around $180–$250 per night

The Shasta Inn combines a cozy, rustic charm with touches of luxury, making it a great option for travelers seeking a unique stay. With wooden beams, stone fireplaces, and large, comfortable beds, the rooms feel like a blend between a mountain lodge and a boutique hotel. I stayed here during fall, and the warmth of the interiors made it feel like a second home. Their staff goes above and beyond to ensure you have everything you need, and they're always ready with tips on hidden spots to explore around town.

C. Budget-Friendly Hotels

For budget-conscious travelers, Mount Shasta has plenty of affordable options that don't skimp on comfort. These budget-friendly hotels offer clean, comfortable rooms and convenient locations for exploring the area.

Strawberry Valley Inn

Location: 1142 S Mount Shasta Blvd, Mt Shasta, CA 96067

Price: Starting at $90 per night

Strawberry Valley Inn is one of my go-to choices when I'm looking to keep things simple and affordable. With its colorful, retro-style decor and welcoming vibe, this place is charming in a unique way. The rooms are clean, cozy, and equipped with all the basics, plus a few extras like complimentary coffee and a small outdoor seating area. One of my favorite things here is the friendly atmosphere; the owners are often around and happy to chat or share recommendations. This inn is close to downtown, making it easy to explore shops, restaurants, and nearby hiking trails without a car.

A-1 Choice Inn

Location: 1340 S Mount Shasta Blvd, Mt Shasta, CA 96067

Price: Rates start around $70–$100 per night

The A-1 Choice Inn is a simple, no-frills option that's ideal for travelers on a tight budget. This motel offers clean, basic rooms with a comfortable bed and a quiet atmosphere. I stayed here once on a solo trip, and while it lacks the charm of the higher-end options, it's a reliable place to rest your head after a long day of exploring. It's also located close to town, so you're never far from local amenities and attractions.

D. Boutique Guesthouses

Boutique guesthouses in Mount Shasta offer a personalized experience, often with unique decor and a cozy, welcoming vibe. These places are ideal for travelers looking for something a bit different, with a more intimate feel than a traditional hotel.

Shasta Starr Ranch

Location: 1008 W A Barr Rd, Mt Shasta, CA 96067

Price: Around $150–$200 per night

Staying at Shasta Starr Ranch is like stepping back in time. This Victorian-style guesthouse is charmingly decorated with vintage furniture, giving it a classic, cozy atmosphere. I stayed here during the summer, and the garden was in full bloom, with flowers adding a beautiful pop of color around the property. Each room has its own character, and the common areas have a library and comfortable seating, making it feel like you're staying in a home rather than a hotel. Breakfast here is a real treat, with homemade pastries and local ingredients that make every morning special.

Cold Creek Inn

Location: 724 N Mount Shasta Blvd, Mt Shasta, CA 96067

Price: Starting at $100 per night

Cold Creek Inn is another fantastic boutique option that's known for its friendly service and relaxed atmosphere. The rooms have a simple, rustic decor with wood accents that blend well with the natural surroundings. I stayed here during a winter visit, and the snow-capped view of Mount Shasta from my room was breathtaking. Cold Creek Inn also has a small outdoor seating area, perfect for morning coffee as you watch the sunrise over the mountains.

E. Unique Stays

For those looking for something out of the ordinary, Mount Shasta has several unique accommodation options that allow you to experience the area in a whole new way.

The McCloud River Mercantile Hotel

Location: 241 Main St, McCloud, CA 96057

Price: Rooms range from $125 to $300 per night, depending on the theme.

This historic hotel in the nearby town of McCloud offers themed rooms, each designed to reflect a different era or style. I stayed in the "Railroad Room," which is decorated with vintage train memorabilia, a nod to the town's history as a railroad hub. The hotel has a charming Old West feel, and it's close to McCloud Falls, making it a convenient base for exploring the area. Each room has its own theme, and staying here feels like you're stepping into a different time period.

Yurts and Cabins at Castle Lake

If you're looking for a more rustic, nature-oriented experience, consider renting a yurt or cabin near Castle Lake. These rentals are perfect for those wanting a closer connection to nature without fully roughing it. The yurts are cozy and equipped with basic amenities, while the cabins offer more space and comfort. I spent a weekend in a cabin by Castle Lake, and it was magical to wake up each morning surrounded by trees, with the lake just a short walk away.

F. Top Recommended Accommodation

If I had to choose one place to recommend, it would be the Mount Shasta Ranch Bed and Breakfast. Located just outside town, this charming bed and breakfast has everything you need for a relaxing stay: beautiful decor, comfortable rooms, and a warm, inviting atmosphere. The owners are incredibly welcoming and have a wealth of knowledge about the area, making them a fantastic resource for first-time visitors. Breakfast here is an experience in itself, with homemade jams, fresh pastries, and locally sourced ingredients.

G. Choosing the Right Accommodation for You

Choosing the right place to stay depends on what kind of experience you're looking for. For those wanting a luxurious retreat with all the amenities, Mount Shasta Resort is an excellent choice. If you're on a budget or prefer a simpler experience, budget-friendly options like Strawberry Valley Inn or A-1 Choice Inn offer comfort without breaking the bank.

For a unique experience, boutique guesthouses like Shasta Starr Ranch offer a cozy, welcoming vibe, perfect for those who enjoy a more personalized stay. I've stayed in a range of places, and each one has added a different dimension to my trips, from the luxurious comfort of the resort to the rustic charm of the yurts by Castle Lake.

H. Booking Tips and Tricks

To make the most of your stay, it's best to book early, especially if you're planning to visit during peak season. Summer and winter are particularly busy, and the most popular spots fill up quickly. When booking online, check for last-minute deals or packages that might include discounted rates or additional perks.

If you're visiting for a longer stay, consider reaching out directly to the accommodation. Some places offer extended-stay discounts, and you might even score a better rate by calling and speaking with the staff. I've had luck with this approach a few times, especially when booking for a week or more.

Summary

This chapter provides a comprehensive guide to Mount Shasta's accommodation options, from luxury resorts to budget-friendly motels, unique boutique guesthouses, and rustic yurts. Whether you're here for a romantic getaway, a family trip, or a solo adventure, there's a perfect place to rest your head after a day of exploring. Each accommodation offers its own experience, and with this guide, you're well-prepared to choose the one that best fits your needs.

Chapter 8

Dining and Local Cuisine

Mount Shasta may be a small town, but it has a vibrant and diverse food scene that offers something for everyone, from cozy cafes to high-end restaurants and locally-sourced cuisine. I've made it a point to explore as many dining spots as possible here, and each place has its own charm and character. Here's a guide to the best places to eat, complete with personal favorites and insider tips to help you savor the local flavors.

Top-Rated Restaurants in Town

When it comes to dining in Mount Shasta, there are several must-visit spots that consistently deliver fantastic food and warm, welcoming service. Here are a few of my top picks:

Lily's Restaurant

Location: 1013 S Mount Shasta Blvd, Mt Shasta, CA 96067

Cuisine: Organic, farm-to-table American

Lily's Restaurant is a gem in the heart of Mount Shasta. This cozy spot is known for its organic, locally-sourced ingredients and delicious, hearty dishes. I always stop by for breakfast or brunch when I'm in town. My go-to order is the smoked salmon scramble with fresh herbs—it's flavorful and perfectly cooked every time. The staff here are incredibly friendly, and there's a warmth to the place that makes you feel right at home. Lily's also has a beautiful outdoor seating area, which is perfect on a sunny day with views of the mountain in the distance.

Pipeline Craft Taps & Kitchen

Location: 311 N Mount Shasta Blvd, Mt Shasta, CA 96067

Cuisine: American, pub food, with a focus on craft beer

Pipeline Craft Taps & Kitchen is the spot to be if you're a fan of craft beer and hearty pub food. With a rotating selection of local and regional beers on tap, this place is a favorite for both locals and travelers.

The food is equally impressive—the trout tacos are a standout, made with fresh-caught trout and topped with a tangy slaw. I remember one night here after a long hike, enjoying a cold beer and a plate of loaded nachos with friends. The atmosphere is relaxed, the food is filling, and the staff are always happy to offer recommendations.

Bistro 107

Location: 107 Chestnut St, Mt Shasta, CA 96067

Cuisine: Italian-inspired dishes and fine dining

If you're in the mood for a more upscale experience, Bistro 107 is the place to go. This intimate restaurant specializes in Italian-inspired dishes with a local twist. On my last visit, I tried the wild mushroom risotto, and it was divine—the flavors were rich and earthy, perfectly balanced with fresh herbs. Bistro 107 also has a great selection of wines, making it an ideal spot for a romantic dinner or a special occasion. Be sure to make a reservation, as this place fills up quickly, especially on weekends.

Local Dishes to Try

Mount Shasta has a few local specialties that you won't want to miss. Here are some dishes that capture the essence of this mountain town:

Trout Dishes

With nearby lakes like Lake Siskiyou and rivers teeming with fish, fresh-caught trout is a staple in many restaurants. Pipeline Craft Taps & Kitchen's trout tacos are a unique take, combining local ingredients with a Tex-Mex twist. Another great option is the trout fillet at Lily's, served with seasonal vegetables and a lemon-butter sauce that perfectly complements the fish's natural flavors. I always make it a point to order trout when I'm here, as it's both delicious and a true taste of Mount Shasta's natural bounty.

Grass-Fed Beef

Several restaurants in the area pride themselves on using grass-fed, locally-sourced beef. At Bistro 107, the grass-fed beef burger is a standout, served with caramelized onions, sharp cheddar, and a side of crispy fries. It's hearty and flavorful, with a freshness that's hard to find in typical burgers. The beef is tender and juicy, and you can really taste the quality of the ingredients.

Vegan and Vegetarian Options

Mount Shasta has a surprising variety of vegan and vegetarian-friendly options. As someone who often opts for plant-based meals, I've enjoyed exploring these spots over the years.

Seven Suns Coffee & Cafe

Location: 1011 S Mount Shasta Blvd, Mt Shasta, CA 96067

Cuisine: Vegetarian-friendly cafe fare

Seven Suns Coffee & Cafe is a staple for breakfast or a light lunch, offering vegetarian and vegan options that are both delicious and filling. I usually go for their veggie wrap, loaded with fresh greens, avocado, and a tangy dressing. It's light but satisfying, and pairs perfectly with one of their strong, aromatic lattes. Seven Suns is a cozy spot with a laid-back atmosphere, and it's always filled with locals and travelers alike.

Maruti Indian & Organic Restaurant

Location: 531 Chestnut St, Mt Shasta, CA 96067

Cuisine: Indian, organic, vegetarian

Maruti Indian & Organic Restaurant is a fantastic option for vegetarian and vegan diners, offering a variety of Indian dishes made with organic ingredients. Their vegan-friendly masala dosa is a favorite of mine, filled with spiced potatoes and served with a coconut chutney that's creamy and flavorful. The restaurant's commitment to organic, locally-sourced ingredients makes it stand out, and you can taste the freshness in every dish.

Cafes and Coffee Shops

There's no shortage of cozy coffee spots in Mount Shasta, each with its own personality and style. Whether you're looking to grab a quick espresso or settle in with a book and a cappuccino, these cafes are worth a visit.

Seven Suns Coffee & Cafe

I've mentioned Seven Suns before, but it's worth repeating—it's the best spot for a casual coffee experience in town. They offer a variety of espresso drinks, teas, and pastries, and their baristas are skilled at making a perfectly balanced latte. I love stopping here in the morning before heading out for a hike, grabbing a coffee to go along with one of their homemade muffins.

Mt. Shasta Pastry

Location: 305 N Mt Shasta Blvd, Mt Shasta, CA 96067

Cuisine: Bakery and coffee shop

Mt. Shasta Pastry is a bakery and cafe that specializes in fresh pastries, sandwiches, and coffee. I highly recommend their almond croissants—they're flaky, buttery, and filled with a rich almond paste. The cafe is a small, inviting space with a warm ambiance, making it an ideal spot to relax with a cup of coffee and a pastry after a morning hike. Their quiches are also fantastic if you're looking for something savory.

Farm-to-Table and Organic Dining

Mount Shasta's proximity to local farms and its community's focus on sustainability have fostered a strong farm-to-table culture. Many restaurants here prioritize organic, locally-sourced ingredients, which adds a distinct freshness to their dishes.

The Garden Tap

Location: 1222 S Mount Shasta Blvd, Mt Shasta, CA 96067

Cuisine: Organic, farm-to-table

The Garden Tap is a newer addition to Mount Shasta's dining scene, and it has quickly become one of my favorite places. Their menu changes with the seasons, as they source ingredients directly from local farms. During my last visit, I had a roasted vegetable bowl with quinoa, fresh greens, and a house-made tahini dressing. The flavors were vibrant, and knowing that everything on my plate was sourced nearby added an extra layer of enjoyment. Their outdoor seating area, surrounded by plants and flowers, makes for a peaceful dining experience.

Wayside Grill

Location: 400 N Mount Shasta Blvd, Mt Shasta, CA 96067

Cuisine: American, farm-to-table

Wayside Grill offers a blend of classic American dishes with a farm-to-table twist. Their salads are especially noteworthy, made with greens and vegetables from local farms. I tried the seasonal grilled vegetable salad, topped with a lemon vinaigrette, and it was both fresh and satisfying. The restaurant has a welcoming, family-friendly atmosphere, making it a great spot for a relaxed dinner after a day of exploring.

Self-Catering and Grocery Options

For those who prefer to cook their own meals, Mount Shasta has several grocery stores and markets offering fresh, local ingredients.

Berryvale Grocery

Location: 305 S Mount Shasta Blvd, Mt Shasta, CA 96067

Offerings: Organic produce, bulk foods, local products

Berryvale Grocery is a haven for anyone looking to stock up on organic and natural foods. This small but well-stocked store has a great selection of fresh produce, bulk items, and specialty products like locally-made cheeses and breads. I often stop here to pick up picnic supplies or ingredients for a simple meal. The store also has a small deli with grab-and-go items, perfect for a quick lunch before hitting the trails.

Mount Shasta Farmers' Market

Location: Downtown Mount Shasta, open seasonally

Offerings: Fresh produce, artisan products, baked goods

If you're in town during the summer, the Mount Shasta Farmers' Market is a fantastic place to experience the local food scene. Held in downtown Mount Shasta, this market features local farmers, artisans, and bakers selling everything from fresh fruits and vegetables to handmade soaps and jams. I love wandering through the market, sampling fresh berries and chatting with the vendors. It's a lively community event that showcases the best of Mount Shasta's local flavors.

Summary

Mount Shasta's dining scene offers a surprising variety of options, from organic cafes to fine dining and local specialties. Whether you're a food lover, a vegan, or simply someone who enjoys a good meal, this town has something to offer. Each place I've listed brings a unique touch to the area's culinary offerings, and this guide will help you savor the flavors of Mount Shasta to the fullest.

Chapter 9

Shopping and Souvenirs

Mount Shasta may be best known for its natural beauty, but the shopping scene here is a hidden gem. From unique boutiques and outdoor gear shops to local artisan stores, there's something special about picking up a memento from this scenic mountain town. I've spent countless afternoons browsing the shops, and it's always a pleasure to find items that reflect the spirit of Mount Shasta. Here's a guide to some of my favorite places to shop for souvenirs, local crafts, and essential gear.

Unique Shops and Boutiques

Mount Shasta's unique boutiques are a delight for anyone who loves exploring one-of-a-kind stores. Many of these shops feature items that capture the town's spiritual side, as well as its connection to nature and adventure.

Soul Connections

Location: 321 N Mount Shasta Blvd, Mt Shasta, CA 96067

Soul Connections is a must-visit for anyone interested in the mystical and spiritual aspects of Mount Shasta. This metaphysical shop is filled with crystals, incense, essential oils, and books on spiritual topics. On my first visit, I picked up a beautiful obsidian stone—a piece that reminds me of Mount Shasta's volcanic origins. The shop also offers readings and energy healing sessions for those interested in exploring the mountain's spiritual reputation more deeply.

The staff at Soul Connections are incredibly knowledgeable and always eager to help customers find items that resonate with them. Even if you're not typically drawn to metaphysical shops, it's worth visiting just to see the unique selection and learn about the spiritual culture that draws so many people to Mount Shasta.

Mount Shasta Gifts

Location: 314 N Mount Shasta Blvd, Mt Shasta, CA 96067

If you're looking for traditional souvenirs, Mount Shasta Gifts is the place to go. This shop offers a wide variety of Mount Shasta-themed items, from T-shirts and postcards to locally crafted candles and keychains. I've picked up several items here over the years, including a quirky Mount Shasta magnet that always gets comments when people see it on my fridge. The shop has something for every budget, so it's perfect for finding gifts for friends and family back home.

Local Art and Crafts

Mount Shasta is home to many talented artists, and local galleries and craft shops showcase their work beautifully. Supporting these artisans is a wonderful way to take home a piece of Mount Shasta's creative spirit.

Gallery 555

Location: 555 N Mount Shasta Blvd, Mt Shasta, CA 96067

Gallery 555 is a small but impressive gallery featuring artwork by local and regional artists. The pieces here range from paintings and photography to sculpture and ceramics, all inspired by the beauty of Mount Shasta and the surrounding landscapes. I purchased a small watercolor painting of the mountain from Gallery 555, and it's now one of my favorite pieces at home. Every time I look at it, I'm reminded of the serenity and beauty of the area.

The gallery staff are friendly and knowledgeable, often sharing stories about the artists and their inspirations. It's a great place to find a unique, high-quality souvenir that truly captures the essence of Mount Shasta.

Outdoor Gear Stores

For those planning to spend a lot of time outdoors, Mount Shasta's outdoor gear stores are essential stops. These shops not only carry top-notch equipment but are also staffed by locals who know the area well and can offer invaluable advice on trails, weather conditions, and gear.

The Fifth Season

Location: 300 N Mount Shasta Blvd, Mt Shasta, CA 96067

The Fifth Season is an iconic outdoor store that has everything you need for exploring Mount Shasta and the surrounding wilderness. From hiking boots and climbing gear to snowshoes and skis, this shop is a one-stop solution for outdoor enthusiasts. I've rented equipment here multiple times, and each experience has been smooth and easy. The staff are seasoned adventurers themselves, so they can recommend the best gear for your planned activities.

One of the things I love about The Fifth Season is their rental program. You can rent gear for a day or a week, and it's a great way to try out equipment before committing to a purchase. Whether you're climbing, skiing, or hiking, this store has you covered.

Shasta Base Camp

Location: 308 S Mount Shasta Blvd, Mt Shasta, CA 96067

Shasta Base Camp is another fantastic spot for outdoor gear, particularly for climbing and biking enthusiasts. This shop has a laid-back vibe, and the staff are incredibly helpful. They also offer guided tours, which I joined on one occasion to explore some of the lesser-known trails. It was an incredible experience, and I highly recommend it if you want a more personalized adventure.

Best Places to Buy Souvenirs

If you're looking for classic Mount Shasta souvenirs, there are a few spots that consistently offer quality items at reasonable prices. These shops are perfect for picking up mementos that will remind you of your time here.

Crystal Keepers

Location: 206 N Mount Shasta Blvd, Mt Shasta, CA 96067

Crystal Keepers is another metaphysical store that focuses specifically on crystals and gemstones. This shop has an impressive selection of crystals, from small pocket stones to large geodes. I picked up a piece of amethyst here on one visit, and it has since become a treasured item in my home. The staff are very knowledgeable about the properties of each stone, and they're happy to help you find something that resonates with you.

Shambhala Center

Location: 320 N Mount Shasta Blvd, Mt Shasta, CA 96067

The Shambhala Center is a holistic store offering everything from yoga mats to incense, along with a variety of Mount Shasta-themed souvenirs. This shop is a great place to find items that blend practicality with spirituality. I bought a meditation cushion here that I use regularly, and it always reminds me of my time in Mount Shasta. They also have a lovely selection of Mount Shasta T-shirts, which make great gifts.

Shopping Tips and Bargain Finds

Shopping in Mount Shasta is a mix of discovering unique finds and supporting local businesses. Here are some tips to help you make the most of your shopping experience:

Visit During Sales and Events: Mount Shasta hosts occasional events and sales where local vendors offer discounts on unique items. For example, the annual community yard sale in summer is a great opportunity to find vintage pieces, handmade crafts, and even outdoor gear at bargain prices. I found a beautiful handcrafted bracelet here one year, and it's still one of my favorite accessories.

Ask About Local Artisans: Many stores, especially the boutiques and art galleries, feature work from local artists and craftspeople. If you're looking for a special piece, ask the staff about the artists they work with. I've found that these items often come with a story, adding an extra layer of meaning to your purchase.

Check Out Pop-Up Shops: During the summer months, Mount Shasta often has pop-up markets where artisans sell jewelry, pottery, clothing, and other handmade goods. These markets are a great place to find unique, limited-edition items directly from the people who made them. I bought a beautiful, hand-painted mug from one such pop-up market, and it's now my favorite mug to use in the mornings.

Additional Shopping Spots for Outdoor Enthusiasts

For those planning on spending a lot of time in nature, the right gear can make all the difference. I highly recommend exploring the local outdoor stores to find what you need.

Mountain High Coffee and Gear

Location: 210 N Mount Shasta Blvd, Mt Shasta, CA 96067

This combination coffee shop and gear store is a great place to pick up last-minute supplies. From camping essentials to sturdy footwear, they have a solid selection of items for the casual explorer. Plus, you can grab a coffee while you shop! I discovered this place on a chilly morning and was thrilled to find both a warm jacket and a hot espresso waiting for me.

Summary

Shopping in Mount Shasta offers a delightful mix of practicality, spirituality, and creativity. Whether you're looking for a unique souvenir, high-quality outdoor gear, or a special gift, this town has a little bit of everything. I hope this guide helps you find the perfect mementos to remember your visit, and perhaps a few treasures that you'll cherish for years to come.

Now let's move on to Chapter 10: Health and Wellness in Mount Shasta. I'll keep the same detailed, engaging style to ensure a comprehensive experience for each chapter. Let's dive into Mount Shasta's wellness options, from yoga and meditation to spas and holistic health practices.

Chapter 10

Health and Wellness in Mount Shasta

Mount Shasta is known not only for its natural beauty but also for its reputation as a wellness destination. This town attracts people from all walks of life who are looking to unwind, recharge, and find balance in mind, body, and spirit. With a variety of wellness centers, spas, and holistic practices, Mount Shasta offers an incredible environment for health and healing. I've taken advantage of many of these offerings over the years, and each visit leaves me feeling refreshed and more connected to the peaceful energy of the area. Here's a guide to Mount Shasta's best wellness experiences, complete with insights and tips to help you make the most of your time here.

Local Spas and Retreats

Mount Shasta's spas and wellness retreats offer a range of services, from massages and facials to natural mineral baths. Many of these places focus on holistic wellness, incorporating practices that balance both body and mind.

Stewart Mineral Springs

Location: 4617 Stewart Springs Rd, Weed, CA 96094

Prices: $25–$60 for mineral baths, additional fees for other treatments

Stewart Mineral Springs is one of the most popular wellness spots in the area, and for good reason. This peaceful retreat, located just outside of Mount Shasta, is known for its natural mineral baths, which are believed to have healing properties. I first visited Stewart Mineral Springs during a winter trip, and soaking in the warm mineral waters while surrounded by snow-covered trees was a magical experience. The water is rich in minerals like magnesium and calcium, which can help soothe sore muscles and relax the body.

In addition to the mineral baths, Stewart Mineral Springs offers a variety of spa services, including massages and saunas. One of their unique treatments is the wood-fired sauna followed by a cold plunge in the nearby river. It's an intense experience, but incredibly invigorating. The combination of hot and cold therapy left me feeling recharged, and I highly recommend it for anyone looking to experience something a little different.

Sacred Mountain Spa

Location: 201 N Mount Shasta Blvd, Mt Shasta, CA 96067

Prices: Massage services range from $80 to $150, with packages available

Sacred Mountain Spa is a cozy, welcoming spa right in the heart of Mount Shasta. This spa focuses on holistic healing practices, including aromatherapy, Reiki, and deep tissue massage. I had a 90-minute aromatherapy massage here, and it was one of the most relaxing experiences I've ever had. The therapist used a blend of essential oils tailored to my needs, and the entire session felt personalized and nurturing.

The spa's interior is decorated with calming colors and soft lighting, creating a peaceful atmosphere that makes you feel at ease the moment you walk in. They also offer skincare services, such as facials and body treatments, which are great for anyone looking to pamper themselves.

Yoga and Meditation Centers

Yoga and meditation are central to Mount Shasta's wellness culture. Several studios offer classes for all levels, along with meditation workshops and wellness events that create a strong sense of community.

Mount Shasta Yoga Center

Location: 118 Siskiyou Ave, Mt Shasta, CA 96067

Prices: Drop-in classes are around $15; multi-class packages are available

The Mount Shasta Yoga Center is a serene and welcoming space that offers classes for everyone, from beginners to experienced yogis. The first class I attended here was a gentle Hatha session, and it left me feeling grounded and connected to the energy of the mountain. The studio itself has large windows that let in plenty of natural light, and on clear days, you can even see Mount Shasta in the distance as you practice.

One of my favorite experiences here was a weekend yoga and meditation workshop. The instructors guided us through various techniques for mindfulness and breathwork, and it was a powerful experience. The sense of calm I felt at the end of the workshop stayed with me for days, making this yoga center a place I always return to when I'm in town.

Shasta Yoga Institute

Location: 224 Red Fir Loop, Mt Shasta, CA 96067

Prices: Drop-in classes are around $18

The Shasta Yoga Institute offers a range of classes, from traditional Hatha and Vinyasa to more specialized practices like restorative yoga and Qi Gong. I joined a restorative yoga class here after a long day of hiking, and it was exactly what I needed to release tension and recharge. The institute also hosts meditation workshops and sound healing events, which are wonderful for those seeking a deeper spiritual experience.

The instructors at Shasta Yoga Institute are knowledgeable and approachable, creating a safe space for both beginners and experienced practitioners. The studio itself is intimate, with a warm and inviting ambiance that makes it easy to relax and focus on your practice.

Natural Healing and Holistic Practices

Mount Shasta has a strong community of holistic healers offering services that range from energy healing to herbal medicine. These practices are deeply rooted in the town's spiritual culture, and they provide a unique way to explore wellness from a different perspective.

Shasta Vortex Adventures

Location: 501 N Mount Shasta Blvd, Mt Shasta, CA 96067

Prices: Vary depending on service; tours and energy healings range from $100 to $200

Shasta Vortex Adventures is known for its spiritual and energy healing services, drawing visitors who seek a deeper connection to the mountain's mystical reputation. They offer a variety of services, including energy healing, guided meditation, and spiritual tours. During one visit, I signed up for a vortex tour, which took us to several energy-rich sites around the mountain. Our guide shared fascinating stories about the area's spiritual significance, and we even practiced a group meditation in one of the spots.

In addition to tours, Shasta Vortex Adventures offers energy healing sessions, where practitioners use Reiki, sound healing, and crystal therapy to promote relaxation and balance. While energy healing isn't for everyone, it's an interesting experience that offers a unique way to connect with the mountain's energy.

Sacred Valley Healing Center

Location: 202 N Mount Shasta Blvd, Mt Shasta, CA 96067

Prices: Sessions range from $80 to $150

Sacred Valley Healing Center provides a range of holistic services, including acupuncture, herbal medicine, and massage therapy. I tried an acupuncture session here to relieve some lower back pain, and the experience was both calming and effective. The practitioner took the time to understand my needs and tailored the treatment accordingly. By the end of the session, I felt more relaxed and balanced.

The healing center also offers personalized wellness consultations, helping clients incorporate holistic practices into their daily lives. The environment is peaceful and inviting, making it easy to relax and fully immerse yourself in the experience.

Tips for Staying Active

Staying active in Mount Shasta is easy, thanks to the many outdoor activities and wellness-focused facilities available. Here are a few tips to help you maintain a healthy routine during your stay:

Take Advantage of the Trails: Mount Shasta is surrounded by hiking trails for all skill levels, so there's no shortage of places to get in some exercise while enjoying nature. I love starting my mornings with a short hike—nothing clears the mind like a brisk walk surrounded by trees and fresh mountain air.

Join a Yoga Class: Yoga is a popular activity in Mount Shasta, and many studios offer drop-in classes. Even if you're new to yoga, taking a class is a great way to stretch and relax. I always make it a point to join a class or two when I'm here, as it helps me stay centered and balanced.

Use Local Gyms and Fitness Centers: For those who prefer indoor workouts, Mount Shasta has a few fitness centers that offer day passes. Mt. Shasta Health and Fitness Center (633 Lassen Ln, Mt Shasta, CA 96067) has a full range of equipment, including weights, cardio machines, and a pool. It's a great place to get in a workout if you're looking for a more structured exercise routine.

Try Meditation and Breathwork: Mount Shasta's serene environment is perfect for meditation and breathwork practices. Even if you're new to meditation, finding a quiet spot by the lake or in the forest can be a transformative experience. I often bring a small mat and spend some time practicing deep breathing exercises by Lake Siskiyou—just 15 minutes can make a world of difference.

Summary

Mount Shasta's wellness offerings are diverse and rooted in both traditional and holistic practices. Whether you're interested in a relaxing massage, a revitalizing yoga session, or a unique energy healing experience, this town has something for everyone. The combination of natural beauty and a focus on wellness creates an environment where you can truly relax, rejuvenate, and reconnect with yourself. I hope this guide helps you find the wellness experiences that resonate with you and make your time in Mount Shasta even more fulfilling.

Chapter 11

Itineraries for Every Traveler

Mount Shasta has something to offer every type of traveler, whether you're here for a quick weekend escape, a cultural immersion, an adventurous getaway, or a relaxing retreat. Over the years, I've had the pleasure of exploring Mount Shasta in different ways, and each experience has shown me a new side of this beautiful destination. To help you make the most of your time here, I've put together a series of suggested itineraries tailored to various travel preferences.

A. Weekend Getaway

A weekend in Mount Shasta is perfect for a quick escape from the city, offering a balance of relaxation and adventure. Here's a two-day itinerary designed to help you unwind, explore, and savor the highlights of the area.

Day 1: Arrival and Exploration

Morning: Start with breakfast at Seven Suns Coffee & Cafe (1011 S Mount Shasta Blvd), where you can enjoy a strong coffee and a hearty veggie wrap. This cozy cafe is a local favorite and a great place to fuel up for the day.

Late Morning: Head to Lake Siskiyou (41.2786° N, 122.3104° W) for a scenic stroll along the Lake Siskiyou Trail. The 8-mile loop is relatively flat, offering easy access to stunning views of Mount Shasta reflected in the water. If you're short on time, just explore a portion of the trail to get a sense of the lake's beauty.

Afternoon: Enjoy a lakeside picnic with food from Berryvale Grocery (305 S Mount Shasta Blvd), where you can find fresh, organic items. After lunch, consider renting a kayak to paddle around the lake and take in the mountain views from the water.

Evening: For dinner, head to Pipeline Craft Taps & Kitchen (311 N Mount Shasta Blvd) for local craft beers and a satisfying meal. I recommend the trout tacos paired with one of their regional brews.

Day 2: Hiking and Sightseeing

Morning: Start your day with a hike up the Black Butte Trail (41.3625° N, 122.3283° W). This 5.2-mile round trip is moderately challenging, but the views from the top are well worth the effort. Be sure to bring plenty of water and take breaks as needed.

Afternoon: After your hike, unwind with a massage at Sacred Mountain Spa (201 N Mount Shasta Blvd). The spa's relaxing atmosphere and skilled therapists make it the perfect place to rejuvenate before heading home.

B. Cultural Immersion

For those interested in the cultural and spiritual side of Mount Shasta, this itinerary focuses on the area's unique heritage, artistic offerings, and spiritual practices.

Day 1: Art and History

Morning: Begin with a visit to the Sisson Museum (1 N Old Stage Rd), where you can learn about Mount Shasta's history, geology, and the indigenous tribes who first called this place home. The museum's exhibits are both educational and engaging, offering a glimpse into the area's cultural significance.

Afternoon: Explore local art at Gallery 555 (555 N Mount Shasta Blvd), featuring works by regional artists inspired by the landscape. I picked up a small painting here on one visit, and it's now one of my favorite souvenirs from Mount Shasta.

Evening: For dinner, enjoy an organic meal at Lily's Restaurant (1013 S Mount Shasta Blvd). With its emphasis on locally-sourced ingredients, Lily's offers a dining experience that reflects the community's commitment to sustainability and quality.

Day 2: Spiritual Exploration

Morning: Join a vortex tour with Shasta Vortex Adventures (501 N Mount Shasta Blvd), which takes you to energy-rich sites around the mountain. Your guide will share stories about the area's spiritual reputation and lead a group meditation, creating a memorable experience.

Afternoon: End your cultural immersion with a yoga session at the Mount Shasta Yoga Center (118 Siskiyou Ave). The instructors here are welcoming, and the studio offers a serene space to connect with the mountain's energy.

C. Outdoor Adventure

For thrill-seekers and outdoor enthusiasts, this itinerary highlights the best of Mount Shasta's rugged landscapes and outdoor activities.

Day 1: Hiking and Kayaking

Morning: Start with a challenging hike up Castle Dome in Castle Crags State Park (41.1454° N, 122.3177° W). This 6-mile hike offers incredible views of jagged granite peaks and Mount Shasta in the distance.

Afternoon: Head to Lake Siskiyou for an afternoon of kayaking. Rentals are available onsite, and the calm waters provide an ideal setting for paddling and exploring the lake's coves.

Evening: For a hearty dinner, stop by Pipeline Craft Taps & Kitchen for a meal that will refuel you after a day of adventure. The pub's atmosphere is relaxed, and the craft beers are a perfect way to end the day.

Day 2: Climbing and Biking

Morning: If you're up for it, try a guided climb with The Fifth Season (300 N Mount Shasta Blvd), which offers equipment rentals and guided climbing excursions for various skill levels. One summer, I joined a group climb here, and it was an unforgettable experience.

Afternoon: Rent a bike from Shasta Base Camp (308 S Mount Shasta Blvd) and explore the scenic trails around town. The bike trails here are well-maintained, with options for both beginners and experienced riders.

D. Family-Friendly Trip

For families visiting Mount Shasta, this itinerary combines outdoor activities with family-friendly attractions to keep everyone entertained.

Day 1: Lake and Museum Visit

Morning: Begin with a visit to Lake Siskiyou Beach. Kids will love playing in the water, building sandcastles, and spotting wildlife. Pack a picnic and enjoy a leisurely morning by the lake.

Afternoon: Head to the Sisson Museum for a family-friendly learning experience. The exhibits are interactive and designed to engage children, with displays on local history, nature, and even a fish hatchery.

Evening: End the day with a casual dinner at Wayside Grill (400 N Mount Shasta Blvd), which has a relaxed atmosphere and a menu that's sure to please the whole family.

Day 2: Easy Hikes and Ice Cream

Morning: Take an easy hike on the Spring Hill Trail, which is short and offers panoramic views without being too strenuous. It's a perfect trail for younger children or anyone looking for a less challenging walk.

Afternoon: Treat the kids to a sweet treat at Mount Shasta Pastry (305 N Mount Shasta Blvd), which offers a selection of ice creams, pastries, and cookies. The almond croissants are a personal favorite, but the kids will love the wide range of dessert options.

E. Budget Travel

Mount Shasta is a fantastic destination for budget-conscious travelers, with many affordable or free activities that showcase the area's natural beauty.

Day 1: Hiking and Picnicking

Morning: Start with a free hike up the Black Butte Trail, which offers incredible views without any entry fees. Pack your own snacks and water to keep costs down.

Afternoon: Grab affordable picnic supplies at Berryvale Grocery and enjoy lunch at Lake Siskiyou. There's no entrance fee, and you can spend the afternoon swimming, sunbathing, or exploring the lake's shoreline.

Evening: For dinner, consider a budget-friendly meal at Strawberry Valley Inn (1142 S Mount Shasta Blvd), where the food is affordable but still high-quality.

Day 2: Exploring Downtown and Scenic Spots

Morning: Spend the day exploring downtown Mount Shasta. Visit local shops, browse art galleries, and enjoy the laid-back vibe of the town.

Afternoon: Take a scenic drive along Everitt Memorial Highway (41.3086° N, 122.3114° W) for breathtaking views of the mountain and surrounding landscape. This free drive offers multiple pull-off points where you can stop for photos.

F. Solo Traveler's Guide

For solo adventurers, Mount Shasta offers a peaceful, introspective environment that encourages self-discovery and exploration.

Day 1: Hiking and Self-Reflection

Morning: Start with a solo hike on the Panther Meadows Trail (41.3226° N, 122.2115° W), a sacred site known for its peaceful energy. Take time to reflect and enjoy the solitude.

Afternoon: Head to Soul Connections (321 N Mount Shasta Blvd) to browse crystals, books, and spiritual items. I love picking up a small piece from here as a personal reminder of my journey.

Evening: Treat yourself to dinner at Bistro 107 (107 Chestnut St), where the intimate setting makes it a perfect spot for solo travelers.

G. Romantic Getaways

Mount Shasta is an idyllic destination for couples seeking a romantic retreat, offering breathtaking views, cozy accommodations, and peaceful surroundings.

Day 1: Scenic Exploration and Spa Day

Morning: Start your day with a walk around Castle Lake (41.2551° N, 122.3127° W). The scenery is serene, and the lake is a perfect place to relax together.

Afternoon: Book a couple's massage at Sacred Mountain Spa to unwind and enjoy a quiet moment together.

Evening: For dinner, try Mount Shasta Resort's restaurant (1000 Siskiyou Lake Blvd), which offers scenic views and a refined menu. The romantic ambiance makes it an ideal choice for a special evening.

Summary

With these itineraries, Mount Shasta becomes accessible and enjoyable for every type of traveler. Whether you're here for a weekend, a cultural experience, an adventure, or a peaceful retreat, this guide offers a range of personalized suggestions.

Chapter 12

Seasonal Events and Festivals

Mount Shasta's charm goes beyond its natural beauty; the town is also home to a variety of seasonal events and festivals that draw both locals and visitors. From vibrant community parades to spiritually-focused gatherings, each season brings a unique set of celebrations. Attending these events has given me a deeper appreciation for the local culture, and each one offers its own way to connect with the town's welcoming spirit. Here's a guide to some of the best seasonal events and festivals, along with tips for making the most of your experience.

Winter Festivities

Mount Shasta transforms into a winter wonderland during the colder months, making it an ideal setting for cozy and festive gatherings. These events bring warmth and cheer to the chilly season, and there's always a sense of community that makes you feel like part of the celebration.

Shasta Snowfest

When: February

Where: Mount Shasta Ski Park and Downtown Mount Shasta

Shasta Snowfest is a beloved winter event that celebrates the season with a mix of outdoor activities, entertainment, and family-friendly fun. Hosted at the Mount Shasta Ski Park, the event includes skiing and snowboarding competitions, live music, a snowman-building contest, and even a polar plunge for the brave-hearted! I remember my first Snowfest well—it was snowing lightly, and the entire town seemed to glow under the fresh powder.

One of the highlights is the night skiing at the Ski Park, which takes place under twinkling lights and offers an exhilarating way to experience the slopes. If you're new to skiing, Snowfest also has beginner-friendly lessons and guided snowshoe tours. Be sure to bundle up and bring your camera; the festive atmosphere and snow-covered landscapes make for some unforgettable photos.

Holiday Tree Lighting and Caroling

When: December

Where: Downtown Mount Shasta

The holiday season in Mount Shasta wouldn't be complete without the annual tree lighting and caroling event downtown. This gathering brings the community together to celebrate with hot cocoa, holiday treats, and classic carols sung by local choirs. I love joining in on this event, as the lights, music, and smell of pine create a heartwarming holiday atmosphere. If you're in town during December, don't miss this festive celebration—it's a perfect way to experience Mount Shasta's small-town charm.

Spring Celebrations

Spring in Mount Shasta is a time of renewal, with flowers blooming, trails reopening, and the community coming together to celebrate the season. It's a beautiful time to visit, as the fresh, vibrant scenery complements the lively events.

Mount Shasta Earth Day Festival

When: April

Where: Mount Shasta City Park

The Earth Day Festival is a family-friendly event held at Mount Shasta City Park, dedicated to environmental awareness and sustainable living. The festival features live music, eco-friendly vendors, art displays, and workshops on topics like organic gardening, sustainable farming, and renewable energy. I've attended this festival a few times, and it's inspiring to see how passionate the community is about protecting the natural beauty of the area.

There's also a kids' zone with interactive activities, making it a great event for families. Bring a reusable water bottle and take advantage of the free water stations, and don't forget to stop by the booths offering local organic products and handmade crafts.

Summer Festivals

Summer is peak season in Mount Shasta, and the town comes alive with vibrant festivals and outdoor gatherings. It's an ideal time to enjoy warm weather, long days, and the beautiful mountain scenery.

Mount Shasta 4th of July Celebration

When: July 4th

Where: Downtown Mount Shasta and Lake Siskiyou

The 4th of July celebration in Mount Shasta is a classic American experience, complete with a parade, fireworks, and plenty of food and fun. The day starts with a lively parade through downtown, where floats, marching bands, and community groups come together to celebrate Independence Day. I've been lucky enough to attend this event a few times, and the festive energy is infectious.

After the parade, locals and visitors gather at Lake Siskiyou for an afternoon of picnicking, swimming, and relaxing by the water. The day culminates with a spectacular fireworks show over the lake, which is truly magical with Mount Shasta silhouetted in the background. Arrive early to get a good spot by the lake, and bring blankets or chairs for comfort. This celebration is one of Mount Shasta's biggest events of the year, so it's well worth planning your trip around it.

Mount Shasta Music Festival

When: August

Where: Outdoor venues around Mount Shasta

The Mount Shasta Music Festival is a summer highlight, attracting musicians from all over to perform in scenic outdoor venues around town. The festival features a mix of genres, from folk and jazz to rock and blues, with something to suit every musical taste. I attended one year and discovered a fantastic blues band that had everyone up and dancing.

The festival's outdoor settings, including parks and open-air stages with views of the mountain, create a relaxed and enjoyable atmosphere. Many attendees bring picnics, blankets, and chairs to settle in and enjoy the music under the open sky. It's a fantastic way to connect with both the community and the landscape, and it's perfect for anyone who loves live music in a natural setting.

Mount Shasta Lavender Festival

When: June

Where: Local lavender farms around Mount Shasta

Held at local lavender farms, the Mount Shasta Lavender Festival celebrates the beauty and versatility of this fragrant plant. The festival includes tours of the lavender fields, workshops on lavender crafts and cooking, and booths selling everything from lavender-infused lotions to freshly made lavender lemonade. I visited during peak bloom one year, and walking through rows of vibrant purple flowers was like stepping into another world.

The festival also features live music and a variety of local food vendors, making it a lovely way to spend a summer afternoon. Be sure to bring a hat and sunscreen, as the open fields can get quite sunny. If you're a lavender lover, this festival is a must!

Fall Gatherings

As the summer crowds thin out and the leaves begin to change, Mount Shasta celebrates the beauty of autumn with intimate gatherings and reflective events.

Shasta Harvest Festival

When: October

Where: Downtown Mount Shasta

The Shasta Harvest Festival is a celebration of the fall season, with local farmers, artisans, and food vendors coming together to showcase the region's bounty. The festival offers live music, arts and crafts, and seasonal foods like pumpkin pie and apple cider. I attended last year and picked up some homemade jams and hand-carved wooden spoons from local vendors.

This festival has a cozy, small-town feel, and it's a wonderful way to experience the local culture. There are activities for all ages, including face painting and hayrides for the kids, making it a fun day out for families. It's also a great opportunity to stock up on unique, handmade gifts for the holiday season.

Autumn Equinox Celebration

When: September 21

Where: Various spiritual centers around Mount Shasta

The Autumn Equinox Celebration is a more spiritually focused event, observed by several of the town's spiritual and holistic communities. The equinox marks a time of balance and reflection, and many groups hold meditations, ceremonies, and workshops to honor the change of season. I participated in a guided meditation one year, held outdoors with a view of Mount Shasta, and it was a profoundly peaceful experience.

If you're interested in the spiritual side of Mount Shasta, the equinox celebration offers a unique opportunity to connect with like-minded individuals. Many events are open to the public, and you can find information through local wellness centers and spiritual organizations.

Summary

Mount Shasta's seasonal events and festivals are as diverse as the landscape itself, each one offering a unique way to experience the town's culture and community. Whether you're here for a family-friendly celebration, a music festival, or a spiritual gathering, these events are an incredible way to immerse yourself in the local atmosphere. I hope this guide inspires you to join in the festivities and create unforgettable memories in Mount Shasta.

Chapter 13

Practical Information for Visitors

Currency, ATMs, and Credit Cards

In Mount Shasta, the official currency is the U.S. Dollar (USD). Here's what you need to know about handling money:

Currency and Exchange: Most major banks and hotels in larger nearby cities offer currency exchange services. For international visitors, it's best to exchange money before arriving in Mount Shasta, as the town itself may have limited currency exchange options.

ATMs: ATMs are available in various locations around Mount Shasta, including banks, grocery stores, and gas stations. Major banks, such as Wells Fargo and U.S. Bank, have branches here with ATM services. Keep in mind that ATMs may charge withdrawal fees, particularly if you're using an international card.

Credit Cards: Most establishments in Mount Shasta, including restaurants, shops, and hotels, accept major credit cards (Visa, MasterCard, American Express). However, it's wise to carry some cash, as smaller businesses or remote locations may be cash-only.

Medical Facilities and Pharmacies

It's always good to be prepared with local healthcare information:

Medical Facilities: The primary healthcare facility in Mount Shasta is Mercy Medical Center (914 Pine St), which provides emergency services and general medical care. For urgent but non-life-threatening needs, Shasta Regional Medical Center in Redding, approximately an hour's drive south, offers specialized treatment options.

Pharmacies: The Rite Aid Pharmacy (1036 Mt Shasta Blvd) in Mount Shasta stocks prescriptions and over-the-counter medications, first-aid supplies, and basic health essentials. Berryvale Grocery also offers a selection of natural health products, including vitamins, herbal remedies, and organic skincare items.

Mobile Service and Wi-Fi

Staying connected in Mount Shasta can vary, especially in remote areas:

Mobile Service: Verizon, AT&T, and T-Mobile provide the best coverage in Mount Shasta and the surrounding areas. However, signal strength may vary as you move into the mountains or more remote spots. Be aware that higher elevations and trails may have limited or no coverage.

Wi-Fi: Free Wi-Fi is available at many cafes, hotels, and restaurants, including popular spots like Seven Suns Coffee & Cafe. For reliable internet, consider downloading maps or other essentials before heading into areas with spotty coverage.

Language and Useful Phrases

English is the primary language spoken in Mount Shasta. While most locals speak only English, here are a few useful phrases that can help:

"Where's the nearest trailhead?" - Useful for finding the start of local hikes.

"Are there any nearby campsites?" - To ask for camping recommendations.

"Do you have vegetarian/vegan options?" - If you have dietary preferences.

Additionally, if you're visiting local spiritual or ceremonial sites, a polite "Thank you for sharing this sacred space" shows respect for the local culture.

Safety Tips and Emergency Contacts

Safety is paramount, particularly in nature-focused destinations like Mount Shasta. Here are key safety tips and emergency contacts:

Emergency Contacts:

911: For any emergency (police, fire, or medical assistance).

Mercy Medical Center: (530) 926-6111 for hospital services.

Mount Shasta Police Department: (530) 926-7540 for local law enforcement.

Safety Tips:

Weather Preparedness: Weather in Mount Shasta can change quickly, especially at higher elevations. Always check forecasts, dress in layers, and carry rain or snow gear if needed.

Wildlife Awareness: Respect local wildlife by maintaining a safe distance and securing food properly, especially in camping areas.

Trail Safety: Stick to marked trails and let someone know your plans before heading out, especially if exploring alone.

Chapter 14

Best Photo Spots in Mount Shasta

Mount Shasta is a photographer's dream destination, with its dramatic landscapes, diverse wildlife, and mystical ambiance. The mountain, lakes, and natural surroundings provide endless opportunities for capturing breathtaking shots, whether you're a professional photographer or a casual enthusiast. In this chapter, we'll explore some of the best photography spots, tips for capturing unique images, and the important etiquette to respect the environment and other visitors.

Scenic Vistas and Lookouts

One of the most appealing aspects of Mount Shasta is the availability of scenic viewpoints that highlight different sides of the mountain and surrounding landscapes. Here are some must-visit spots:

Lake Siskiyou

Lake Siskiyou is one of the most iconic locations for photographing Mount Shasta. The lake often mirrors the mountain, especially in the calm, early morning hours when the water is undisturbed. Sunrise and sunset are magical times to photograph here, with the mountain bathed in pink and orange hues as the sun rises or sets. I recommend using a wide-angle lens to capture the full scene, including the lake's shoreline and surrounding forest.

Heart Lake

Accessible via a hike from the Castle Lake area, Heart Lake offers a secluded and scenic view of Mount Shasta. From this vantage point, you'll see the mountain framed by the lake in the foreground, creating a perfect composition. I love visiting Heart Lake at sunset—the colors reflect beautifully off the water, and you can catch a serene, elevated view of Mount Shasta's silhouette against the fading light. A tripod and long exposure can help create smooth reflections on the lake, adding to the tranquility of the scene.

Bunny Flat Trailhead

Bunny Flat, located on Everitt Memorial Highway, is a high-elevation lookout that offers panoramic views of the mountain's slopes and surrounding landscapes. This spot is ideal for close-up shots of Mount Shasta's rugged terrain, especially in winter when the peaks are covered in snow. I recommend visiting in spring or early summer when wildflowers are in bloom, adding vibrant colors to your shots. The easy access and breathtaking views make Bunny Flat a popular spot, so try to arrive early to beat the crowds.

Wildlife and Nature Photography

Mount Shasta's rich ecosystem provides ample opportunities for wildlife photography. Here's where you're likely to spot some of the local fauna:

Shasta-Trinity National Forest

Shasta-Trinity National Forest is a vast and diverse area where you can encounter everything from black bears and deer to eagles and smaller birds. Early morning and late evening are prime times for wildlife sightings. Patience is key in wildlife photography—by staying quiet and observant, you increase your chances of capturing animals in their natural behavior. Bring a telephoto lens to maintain a safe distance, and keep in mind that animals may be more visible during quieter hours.

McCloud River Falls

The McCloud River area is known for its beautiful waterfalls and diverse plant and animal life. This location offers opportunities for photographing animals, river habitats, and lush greenery. The river's three waterfalls—Lower, Middle, and Upper Falls—provide dynamic backdrops for long-exposure shots, where the motion of the water contrasts with the stillness of the surrounding forest. A sturdy tripod is essential here, especially for long exposures that capture the waterfalls' energy and motion.

Lake Siskiyou Birdwatching

Lake Siskiyou is an excellent spot for birdwatching, especially early in the morning. Bald eagles, osprey, and other waterfowl are commonly seen here. Bring a long lens (300mm or more) to capture birds in action without disturbing their natural behavior. You'll have the best luck on calm mornings when birds are feeding or nesting around the lake.

Capturing the Northern Lights

On rare occasions, the Northern Lights are visible from Mount Shasta. While sightings are uncommon, being prepared can make all the difference.

Best Conditions: Clear, dark skies with minimal moonlight are ideal for viewing the Northern Lights. Fall and winter are the best seasons for sightings, and areas like Bunny Flat and Heart Lake offer higher elevations with reduced light pollution.

Camera Settings: Set your camera to a high ISO (around 1600–3200) with a wide aperture (f/2.8 or lower) and use a long exposure (10–30 seconds). I use a remote shutter release to avoid camera shake and capture clear, sharp images.

Photography Etiquette

Respecting the environment is crucial when photographing in Mount Shasta. Here are a few key etiquette tips:

Stay on Paths: Avoid trampling vegetation or wandering off trails, especially in fragile ecosystems like the wildflower meadows.

Limit Flash: Flash can disturb both wildlife and fellow visitors, especially in low-light settings. Use natural light whenever possible.

Pack Out Trash: Leave no trace by taking all waste with you, including food wrappers, tripod accessories, and packaging.

Chapter 15

Wildlife and Nature Conservation

Mount Shasta is not only a place of beauty but also a region with rich biodiversity and a delicate ecosystem that requires conservation efforts. In this chapter, we'll explore the unique flora and fauna of the area, endangered species, and how visitors can enjoy Mount Shasta responsibly.

Local Flora and Fauna

The Mount Shasta region is home to diverse species, from towering pines to rare wildflowers and a wide range of animals.

Flora

Ponderosa Pine: These trees are iconic to Mount Shasta's landscape, with tall, straight trunks and needle-like leaves. In early spring, the scent of pine fills the air around the forests, creating a serene atmosphere.

Shasta Lily: This rare wildflower blooms in summer and is known for its striking white and pink flowers. You'll find it in the higher elevations, where it thrives in rocky soil and cooler temperatures.

Manzanita Shrubs: With their distinctive reddish-brown bark and small, waxy leaves, manzanitas add unique texture to the landscape.

Fauna

Black Bears: Though sightings are rare, black bears are present in the forests around Mount Shasta. They're typically shy, but it's essential to store food securely while camping.

Bald Eagles: These majestic birds are often seen around Lake Siskiyou and Shasta-Trinity National Forest. Spotting a bald eagle in flight is a breathtaking experience and a reminder of the region's ecological health.

Mule Deer: Deer are commonly seen grazing in meadows and forests. Early morning is the best time to spot them, often in groups.

Endangered Species Protection

Mount Shasta is home to several endangered and sensitive species, and local conservation efforts focus on preserving their habitats.

Spotted Owl: A threatened species, the spotted owl requires old-growth forests for nesting. Conservation programs focus on maintaining these forests to ensure the owl's survival.

Shasta Crayfish: This is the only crayfish native to California and is critically endangered. It's found in small, isolated springs and creeks, with ongoing efforts to prevent its habitat from being disturbed by human activity.

How to Explore Responsibly

Responsible exploration is crucial for preserving Mount Shasta's natural beauty and wildlife:

Stay on Marked Trails: This minimizes habitat disruption and protects fragile plant life.

Pack Out Trash: Always bring a bag for your trash and pick up litter if you see any.

Respect Wildlife: Observe animals from a distance, especially during nesting or mating seasons.

Conservation Efforts and Volunteer Opportunities

Visitors interested in conservation can contribute to ongoing efforts in several ways:

Volunteer Programs: Organizations like the Shasta-Trinity National Forest offer volunteer opportunities for trail maintenance, invasive species removal, and educational outreach.

Educational Workshops: Local parks and conservation groups host workshops on topics like native plant identification, wildlife protection, and eco-friendly hiking practices.

Chapter 16

A Guide to Spiritual Exploration

Mount Shasta has long been considered a spiritual hub, attracting visitors from around the world who seek mystical experiences and deeper connections with nature. This chapter provides an overview of sacred sites, legends, spiritual retreats, and respectful practices for those seeking spiritual enrichment.

Sacred Sites and Ceremonies

Mount Shasta is home to sacred sites and is deeply connected to Native American traditions. Here's where to experience the mountain's spiritual energy:

Panther Meadows

Panther Meadows is considered one of the most sacred areas on Mount Shasta, often visited by those seeking peace and spiritual connection. Visitors are encouraged to walk respectfully and to stay on paths, as the meadows are fragile and hold deep significance for the local indigenous tribes.

Vision Quest Locations

Some visitors come to Mount Shasta for a vision quest—a spiritual journey to seek personal insight or growth. Local guides and spiritual organizations offer structured vision quests, often including meditation and solitude in nature.

Local Legends and Mystical Stories

Mount Shasta is associated with numerous legends and mystical stories, many involving ancient civilizations or spiritual beings:

The Lemurian Legend: According to legend, an ancient race known as the Lemurians lives within the mountain in a hidden city called Telos. Believers say that the Lemurians are spiritually advanced beings, and many

visitors come to meditate and connect with their energy.

Saint Germain Sightings: Some claim to have seen Saint Germain, an ascended master, on the slopes of Mount Shasta. His presence is believed to guide spiritual seekers toward enlightenment.

Visiting the Lemurian Caves

For those intrigued by the legend of the Lemurians, local guides sometimes offer exploratory trips to caves around Mount Shasta. While there's no verified evidence of Lemurian civilization, exploring these caves offers a unique and mystical experience.

Spiritual Retreats and Meditation

Several retreat centers and spiritual organizations offer programs and workshops in Mount Shasta:

Shasta Abbey: A Zen Buddhist monastery open to visitors for meditation and spiritual study. It provides a peaceful environment for reflection and inner peace.

Retreat Centers: Various centers around Mount Shasta offer guided meditations, Reiki, energy healing, and yoga sessions. These retreats provide a chance to unplug, focus on inner growth, and connect with Mount Shasta's unique spiritual energy.

Chapter 17

What to Do and What Not to Do in Mount Shasta

Mount Shasta is an extraordinary destination, blending natural beauty, spiritual significance, and vibrant local culture. However, like any special place, it has unique customs, guidelines, and etiquette that visitors should be mindful of. By understanding and respecting these local practices, visitors can fully enjoy their time in Mount Shasta while preserving the integrity and beauty of the area for future travelers. Here's a guide on what you should and shouldn't do while exploring Mount Shasta, covering environmental, cultural, and social considerations.

Respecting Local Culture and Traditions

Mount Shasta holds deep significance for both indigenous cultures and spiritual communities. Being aware of these cultural elements is essential to having a respectful and enriching experience.

Understanding Indigenous Significance

The indigenous peoples, particularly the Wintu and other Native American tribes, consider Mount Shasta a sacred place. Panther Meadows, for example, is a site of great spiritual importance. As a visitor, it's crucial to treat such areas with the reverence they deserve. Avoid loud noises, respect any posted signs, and stay on designated trails to protect these fragile ecosystems. Local indigenous communities sometimes conduct ceremonies here, and if you encounter one, observe respectfully from a distance without taking photos or recording.

Participating in Local Ceremonies with Respect

Some spiritual events or ceremonies open to the public may require a specific mindset or level of respect. If you choose to participate, follow any guidance provided by facilitators, such as refraining from conversation during meditation, leaving cell phones off, or removing shoes in certain areas. When I joined a group meditation here, the guide asked everyone to focus on breathing and avoid conversation, allowing for a more profound and uninterrupted experience for all.

Environmental Do's and Don'ts

Mount Shasta's ecosystems are diverse but sensitive. Following environmental best practices is essential to preserving the area's natural beauty and ecological health.

Do Stay on Marked Trails

Sticking to designated trails not only ensures your safety but also helps protect delicate flora and habitats. In areas like Panther Meadows, where wildflowers and rare plants grow, veering off-trail can lead to soil erosion and damage to vegetation. Walking only on marked paths preserves the environment and protects fragile plant life.

Do Practice Leave No Trace Principles

The Leave No Trace philosophy encourages minimizing our impact on the environment. Bring reusable water bottles and bags, pack out all trash (including organic waste like food scraps), and avoid picking flowers or taking rocks from natural sites. I make it a habit to bring a small bag for any litter I encounter on trails, helping to keep the area clean for others.

Don't Disturb Wildlife

Mount Shasta is home to a variety of animals, from deer and birds to the occasional black bear. Observing wildlife from a distance is a must. Approaching or feeding animals can alter their behavior, harm their health, and create unsafe situations. Use binoculars or a zoom lens to appreciate animals without intruding on their space.

Don't Build Cairns or Alter Natural Features

While stacking rocks or building cairns may seem harmless, it can disrupt natural ecosystems and confuse other hikers who rely on cairns as trail markers. Natural features should be left as they are to maintain the landscape's integrity.

Social Etiquette for Visitors

Mount Shasta is a welcoming community, but visitors should still observe a few social etiquette tips to ensure a positive experience for everyone.

Do Support Local Businesses

Supporting locally-owned shops, restaurants, and artisans is a great way to give back to the community. From handmade jewelry to locally-sourced food, Mount Shasta's businesses reflect the region's unique culture and values. The Mount Shasta Farmers' Market is a perfect place to buy local products, meet the people who make them, and contribute directly to the town's economy.

Do Keep Noise Levels Low in Sacred and Natural Areas

In locations like Panther Meadows, Bunny Flat, and other scenic spots, keeping noise to a minimum enhances the tranquility and respectfulness of the environment. These areas are often places of reflection and meditation for both locals and visitors. Avoid playing music on speakers, shouting, or engaging in loud conversations.

Don't Take Photos in Sacred Spaces Without Permission

While Mount Shasta's natural beauty is undoubtedly photogenic, it's essential to ask for permission or refrain from photographing certain sacred sites and ceremonies, especially when indigenous groups or spiritual practitioners are involved. Some places may have restrictions on photography out of respect for cultural or spiritual beliefs.

Don't Engage in Public Display of Artifacts or Cultural Appropriation

Wearing culturally significant attire, like indigenous headdresses or ceremonial jewelry, as a costume can be seen as disrespectful. If you're invited to participate in a cultural ceremony or purchase a piece of indigenous artwork, treat it with respect and avoid treating it as a costume or mere decoration.

Wildlife and Nature Safety

Mount Shasta's wilderness is both beautiful and wild, with certain risks that visitors should be prepared for.

Do Carry Bear Spray and Practice Bear Safety

While bear encounters are rare, being prepared is essential. Carry bear spray if you're hiking in more remote areas and know how to use it. Store all food securely in bear-proof containers when camping, and follow local guidelines for food storage and disposal to avoid attracting bears.

Do Prepare for Rapid Weather Changes

Mount Shasta's weather can change quickly, especially at higher elevations. Bring extra layers, waterproof clothing, and check the forecast before heading out. I always pack a small emergency kit with essentials like a flashlight, extra batteries, a map, and high-energy snacks.

Don't Swim in Unmarked or Dangerous Waters

While lakes like Lake Siskiyou are safe for swimming, other water sources may have unpredictable currents or hidden hazards. Avoid swimming in rivers or ponds without checking for safety signs or warnings. Also, respect "No Swimming" signs, as these are in place for both your safety and the protection of sensitive ecosystems.

Don't Touch or Interact with Potentially Hazardous Plants

Certain plants, such as poison oak, can cause skin irritation or other allergic reactions. It's best to avoid touching any unfamiliar vegetation and wear long sleeves and pants to protect yourself while hiking.

Summary

Understanding the do's and don'ts of Mount Shasta is vital for a respectful and enjoyable visit. By being mindful of local culture, practicing environmental responsibility, respecting social etiquette, and preparing for wilderness safety, you'll contribute to the preservation of this stunning region. Whether you're here for adventure, spiritual exploration, or relaxation, these guidelines will help you connect with Mount Shasta in a way that honors both the land and its people.

Chapter 18

Kid-Friendly Activities

Mount Shasta is an ideal destination for families, with its abundance of outdoor spaces, scenic trails, and educational attractions. From easy hikes that introduce kids to nature to interactive museum exhibits and lakeside activities, there's something here for every young explorer. This chapter provides a comprehensive guide to family-friendly experiences, ensuring a safe, exciting, and enriching visit for all ages.

Family Hikes and Nature Trails

Mount Shasta offers a range of hiking trails that are accessible and enjoyable for families with young children. Here are a few favorites that combine beautiful scenery with easy-to-moderate paths, perfect for introducing kids to the outdoors.

Spring Hill Trail

Difficulty: Easy

Distance: 2.4 miles round-trip

Location: Off Mt Shasta Blvd, near downtown

Spring Hill Trail is a fantastic introductory hike for families. The path is gentle, with a gradual incline that leads to a scenic overlook of Mount Shasta and the surrounding area. Kids will enjoy spotting wildflowers along the way and observing small wildlife like birds and squirrels. At the summit, you'll find panoramic views that make the short hike worth the effort, and there's plenty of space for a family picnic. Bring water and sunscreen, as parts of the trail are exposed.

Castle Lake Trail

Difficulty: Moderate

Distance: 2 miles round-trip to Heart Lake

Location: Castle Lake Rd, about 15 minutes from Mt Shasta City

Castle Lake Trail offers slightly more adventure with its scenic route leading up to Heart Lake. Kids who enjoy exploring rocky terrain will have fun climbing around Castle Lake's shores. The hike to Heart Lake is short but requires some uphill walking, so it's best suited for families with older children. Once you reach Heart Lake, the view of Mount Shasta reflected in the water is breathtaking. On hot days, Castle Lake also has areas where children can safely wade.

McCloud River Falls Trail

Difficulty: Easy to Moderate

Distance: 3.5 miles round-trip to all three falls

Location: McCloud River, about 25 minutes from Mt Shasta City

This trail features three waterfalls—Lower, Middle, and Upper McCloud Falls—along a well-marked path. Each fall offers unique sights and sounds, and kids will be delighted by the rushing water and the chance to explore the riverbanks. Middle Falls, in particular, has an overlook that provides a stunning view of the cascading water. The path between the falls is relatively easy to navigate, with shaded areas that make it suitable for a family outing on warmer days. Pack a picnic to enjoy at one of the designated picnic areas along the river.

Fun Learning at the Sisson Museum

Location: 1 N Old Stage Rd, Mt Shasta, CA 96067

Admission: Free (donations welcome)

The Sisson Museum is a wonderful place for families to explore together, offering a mix of exhibits that are both educational and interactive. The museum covers the history of Mount Shasta, the local indigenous cultures, and the area's natural environment, making it an ideal stop for curious kids.

Kid-Friendly Exhibits

The museum has a dedicated children's area with hands-on exhibits designed to engage young minds. Kids can learn about the region's geology, including Mount Shasta's volcanic history, and explore displays about the area's flora and fauna. There's also a section on the local fish hatchery, where children can learn about the life cycle of trout and even feed the fish at the adjacent hatchery pond—a favorite activity for young visitors.

Seasonal Programs and Events

The Sisson Museum often hosts seasonal events and workshops for families. During the summer, they offer educational programs on topics like forest ecosystems, local wildlife, and environmental stewardship. Check the museum's calendar for upcoming events that might align with your visit.

Lakeside Activities for Children

Mount Shasta's lakes provide a scenic setting for a range of family-friendly activities, from swimming and kayaking to simple lakeside picnics.

Lake Siskiyou Beach and Splash Zone

Location: Lake Siskiyou Camp Resort, 4239 W A Barr Rd, Mt Shasta, CA 96067

Admission: Day-use fee for beach access

Lake Siskiyou Beach is a popular spot for families, with its sandy shoreline and shallow swimming areas that are perfect for children. The lake's calm waters allow for safe swimming and splashing, and kids can build sandcastles on the beach. One of the highlights here is the Splash Zone—a floating water park equipped with slides, trampolines, and climbing structures. The Splash Zone is ideal for kids ages 6 and up, though younger children may also enjoy wading and playing on the shore under supervision.

Kayaking and Paddleboarding

Lake Siskiyou offers kayak and paddleboard rentals, allowing families to explore the lake from the water. The lake's gentle conditions make it suitable for beginners, and children who are comfortable on the water can paddle alongside their parents. Rental facilities provide life jackets, ensuring a safe experience. The view of Mount Shasta from the middle of the lake is stunning, creating a perfect opportunity for family photos.

Fishing at Lake Siskiyou

Fishing is another great activity for families at Lake Siskiyou. Children can try their hand at fishing from the shore or on a rented boat, with the chance to catch rainbow trout and bass. Be sure to check local fishing regulations and get a fishing license if needed. Many families enjoy bringing a small grill to cook their catch for a lakeside picnic—a fun and satisfying way to enjoy a day at the lake.

Interactive Workshops for Kids

Several organizations in Mount Shasta offer interactive workshops and activities that cater to children, making it easy to blend learning with fun.

Mount Shasta Recreation and Parks District Programs

The Mount Shasta Recreation and Parks District often hosts kid-friendly workshops and events, especially during the summer months. From nature walks and outdoor art classes to storytelling sessions, these programs provide children with structured, educational activities. Many programs focus on local wildlife, plant identification, and hands-on nature crafts, encouraging kids to learn about and appreciate the environment.

Art Workshops at Gallery 555

Location: 555 N Mount Shasta Blvd, Mt Shasta, CA 96067

Gallery 555 offers occasional art workshops for children, focusing on nature-inspired themes. Kids can participate in drawing and painting classes, where they'll learn to create art inspired by the landscapes and wildlife of Mount Shasta. These workshops are led by local artists who enjoy sharing their passion with young minds. My niece attended a class here during our last visit, and she left with a beautiful watercolor of Mount Shasta that she proudly displayed at home.

Ranger-Led Junior Ranger Programs

During the summer, the Shasta-Trinity National Forest offers Junior Ranger programs that engage children in exploring nature and learning about the environment. Led by park rangers, these programs include nature hikes, birdwatching, and educational games that introduce kids to topics like ecology, wildlife safety, and conservation. Participants receive Junior Ranger badges, which are a great keepsake to remind them of their experience. Check with the ranger station for schedules and available activities.

Summary

Mount Shasta provides endless opportunities for families to enjoy outdoor adventures, hands-on learning, and quality time together. Whether you're hiking an easy trail, exploring interactive exhibits at the Sisson Museum, or enjoying lakeside fun at Lake Siskiyou, there's something here for every child to enjoy.

Chapter 19

Sustainable Travel Tips

Mount Shasta's natural beauty and unique ecosystem draw countless visitors every year, and sustainable travel practices are essential to preserving this environment for future generations. In this chapter, we'll explore ways to travel responsibly in Mount Shasta, from reducing waste and minimizing your ecological footprint to supporting the local economy. These sustainable travel tips will help you enjoy the area while contributing to its conservation and well-being.

Minimizing Your Environmental Impact

Reducing your impact on the environment is one of the most important aspects of sustainable travel. Here are some simple but effective ways to practice environmental responsibility while visiting Mount Shasta.

Reduce Plastic Waste

Plastic waste is a significant issue worldwide, and even in pristine areas like Mount Shasta, plastic pollution can harm local wildlife and ecosystems. To minimize plastic use, bring a reusable water bottle and refill it at available water stations around town or in parks. I always keep a reusable coffee cup with me as well, which comes in handy at local cafes that offer discounts for bringing your own cup.

Pack Eco-Friendly Toiletries

Opt for eco-friendly, biodegradable toiletries, especially if you're camping or staying in nature-focused accommodations. Soaps, shampoos, and detergents with natural ingredients are better for the environment and help protect local water sources. Look for products that come in recyclable packaging or consider bringing solid toiletries, which last longer and are often more environmentally friendly.

Leave No Trace

The "Leave No Trace" principles are fundamental for anyone visiting natural spaces. This includes packing out all trash, avoiding disturbing wildlife, and respecting nature by not picking plants or disturbing rock formations. When hiking, stay on marked trails to prevent soil erosion and protect sensitive vegetation. I make it a point to pick up any litter I find along trails, leaving the area cleaner than I found it.

Minimize Car Use

While having a car can make it easier to get around Mount Shasta, consider using alternative transportation methods when possible. Mount Shasta's downtown is compact and walkable, making it easy to explore on foot. For longer trips, consider biking or carpooling with other travelers. Electric vehicle (EV) charging stations are available in some areas if you're driving an electric or hybrid vehicle.

Choosing Eco-Friendly Accommodations

Mount Shasta has several accommodation options that prioritize sustainability, making it easier to support eco-conscious businesses. Here are some tips for choosing accommodations that align with sustainable practices.

Stay at Green-Certified Hotels or Eco-Lodges

Look for accommodations with green certifications or eco-friendly initiatives, such as energy-saving practices, waste reduction, and water conservation measures. Many lodges in the area incorporate sustainable practices, like using solar power, offering recycling options, or participating in local conservation efforts.

Opt for Campsites with Minimal Impact Policies

If you're camping, select campsites that follow minimal impact policies and encourage sustainable camping practices. Many campsites near Mount Shasta, including those in Shasta-Trinity National Forest, have strict guidelines on campfires, waste disposal, and water conservation. By following these policies, you help maintain the natural beauty and health of the environment.

Support Locally-Owned Accommodations

Staying at locally-owned accommodations, such as family-run inns or bed-and-breakfasts, supports the local economy and often provides a more personalized experience. Many small, locally-owned lodgings prioritize sustainable practices and are happy to share information on how they contribute to the local community. I've found that staying at family-run inns not only enhances my trip but also helps me connect with the local culture.

Supporting Local Businesses

Supporting local businesses is a great way to reduce your environmental impact and contribute to the local economy. Here's how to shop and dine sustainably in Mount Shasta.

Shop at Farmers' Markets

Mount Shasta has a thriving farmers' market scene where you can buy fresh, locally-sourced produce and handmade products. The Mount Shasta Farmers' Market features fruits, vegetables, baked goods, and artisan crafts made by local vendors. Shopping at the farmers' market reduces food miles and supports local farmers and artisans who use sustainable practices.

Choose Locally-Sourced, Organic Dining Options

Many restaurants in Mount Shasta emphasize locally-sourced, organic ingredients, which are better for the environment and often fresher. Lily's Restaurant is known for its farm-to-table approach, serving dishes made with organic, regional produce. By dining at places that support local farmers, you're contributing to the sustainability of the area's food industry and enjoying a more authentic taste of Mount Shasta's culinary offerings.

Buy Handmade Souvenirs from Local Artisans

When purchasing souvenirs, look for handmade items crafted by local artists, such as jewelry, pottery, or artwork that reflects Mount Shasta's beauty and spirit.

Shops like Gallery 555 and Soul Connections offer unique, locally-made items that make for meaningful mementos. These items not only make great keepsakes but also support local talent and reduce the environmental impact of mass-produced goods.

Responsible Hiking and Camping

Hiking and camping are popular activities in Mount Shasta, but responsible practices are essential to minimize environmental damage. Here's how to explore the outdoors sustainably.

Use Durable Camping Gear

Investing in high-quality, durable camping gear reduces waste and limits your environmental footprint. Choose eco-friendly options like reusable food containers, biodegradable camping supplies, and sustainable clothing made from organic or recycled materials. I also recommend bringing a portable solar charger for small devices, which is a practical and eco-friendly alternative to disposable batteries.

Camp at Designated Sites

Camping only in designated areas helps prevent damage to fragile ecosystems. Shasta-Trinity National Forest and other nearby areas have clearly marked campgrounds designed to minimize environmental impact. Follow all campfire regulations and use established fire rings to prevent wildfires. During dry seasons, campfire restrictions may be in place, so check for updates before your trip.

Practice Responsible Waste Disposal

When camping, pack out all waste, including food scraps, which can attract wildlife. Use biodegradable soap for washing dishes and utensils, and dispose of wastewater at least 200 feet away from water sources. This helps maintain the cleanliness of lakes and rivers, preserving them for other visitors and local wildlife.

Stick to Trails and Avoid Sensitive Areas

When hiking, staying on marked trails is one of the most effective ways to minimize your impact. Veering off paths can harm plant life, cause soil erosion, and disrupt wildlife habitats. In fragile areas like Panther Meadows, even small disturbances can have lasting effects. By sticking to established trails, you're helping to protect these delicate ecosystems.

Additional Tips for Sustainable Travel in Mount Shasta

To wrap up this chapter, here are a few additional tips for eco-friendly travel in Mount Shasta:

Be Water Conscious: Mount Shasta has a delicate water ecosystem, so use water wisely. Take shorter showers, avoid excessive washing of clothes, and refrain from wasting water at campsites.

Avoid Single-Use Items: Bring reusable utensils, bags, and containers to minimize your reliance on disposable items. Many cafes in Mount Shasta also offer incentives for bringing your own coffee cups.

Limit Wildlife Interaction: While it's exciting to see animals up close, remember to respect their space. Feeding animals disrupts their natural behaviors and can make them reliant on human food, which is harmful to their health.

Summary

Sustainable travel practices allow you to enjoy Mount Shasta's beauty while contributing to its preservation. By reducing waste, choosing eco-friendly accommodations, supporting local businesses, and practicing responsible hiking and camping, you help protect this incredible region for generations to come.

Chapter 20

Mount Shasta's Nightlife

Though Mount Shasta is known for its serene mountain landscapes and outdoor adventures, the town has a unique nightlife scene that offers a blend of relaxation, local flavor, and occasional live entertainment. From cozy bars and pubs to special night events under the stars, there's something here for every visitor looking to unwind and enjoy the evening. This chapter explores the top spots and experiences for a memorable night out in Mount Shasta.

Bars and Pubs with Local Brews

Mount Shasta has a few charming bars and pubs that offer a relaxed atmosphere and feature local brews, wines, and creative cocktails. Here's where to head for a cozy evening drink.

Pipeline Craft Taps & Kitchen

Location: 311 N Mount Shasta Blvd, Mt Shasta, CA 96067

Pipeline Craft Taps & Kitchen is a favorite among locals and visitors alike, known for its wide selection of local and regional craft beers. The bar offers a rotating menu of beers on tap, including brews from Northern California and Oregon. I highly recommend trying a flight to sample a few varieties—it's a great way to taste some of the region's best brews. Pipeline's casual vibe and friendly staff make it a great spot to relax after a day of exploring. The pub also offers a menu of delicious comfort foods, like burgers and tacos, perfect for pairing with your drink.

The Vet's Club

Location: 406 N Mt Shasta Blvd, Mt Shasta, CA 96067

The Vet's Club is a longstanding establishment with a retro, dive-bar feel, frequented by locals and visitors looking for an authentic experience. The bar's decor and relaxed atmosphere give it a nostalgic charm, and it's known for its affordable drinks and laid-back vibe. If you're in the mood for a low-key night, The Vet's Club is a great place to grab a beer, chat with locals, and enjoy a slower pace. This spot also has pool tables, making it a fun choice for a casual evening with friends or fellow travelers.

Mount Shasta Brewing Company

Location: 360 College Ave, Weed, CA 96094 (just a short drive from Mt Shasta)

A short drive from Mount Shasta, in the town of Weed, Mount Shasta Brewing Company is a must-visit for craft beer enthusiasts. The brewery offers a range of house-made beers, including the popular Shastafarian Porter and Weed Golden Ale. The tasting room has a warm, rustic ambiance, with views of the brewery's operations. They often host events and tastings, providing a fun, interactive experience. I recommend trying their sampler tray, which lets you taste a variety of their craft brews and find a favorite. They also have a small menu with appetizers and light bites to enjoy with your beer.

Music Venues and Live Performances

For those who enjoy live music, Mount Shasta has a few venues that host performances by local musicians, bands, and touring artists.

Black Bear Diner (Music Nights)

Location: 401 W Lake St, Mt Shasta, CA 96067

Black Bear Diner may be known for its hearty breakfasts and classic American fare, but they also host occasional live music nights. These events feature local musicians playing a range of genres, from folk and jazz to blues and acoustic rock. The diner's warm, welcoming atmosphere makes it an ideal setting for a relaxed evening with good food and music. Check their event schedule for upcoming music nights, as these events can be a great way to experience local talent in a cozy setting.

Mount Shasta Resort (Summer Concert Series)

Location: 1000 Siskiyou Lake Blvd, Mt Shasta, CA 96067

During the summer, Mount Shasta Resort hosts a seasonal concert series that features live music in an outdoor setting overlooking Lake Siskiyou. The concerts typically take place on weekends and include a mix of genres, with bands playing everything from rock and blues to reggae and folk. This event is family-friendly, and visitors are welcome to bring blankets or chairs to sit by the lake while enjoying the music. There's often food and drinks available for purchase, making it easy to settle in for a relaxing evening. The summer concert series is a favorite among locals and provides a scenic, memorable way to spend a night in Mount Shasta.

Seasonal Night Events

Mount Shasta's seasonal events bring a unique nighttime experience, from star-gazing gatherings to festive holiday activities. Here are some annual events to consider if you're visiting during the right season.

Star Gazing Nights at Bunny Flat

Bunny Flat, located at 7,000 feet on the slopes of Mount Shasta, is a prime spot for stargazing, far from city lights and with a clear view of the night sky.

During the summer months, local astronomy groups sometimes host star-gazing events where telescopes are provided, and guides point out constellations, planets, and celestial events. The high elevation and dark skies make this an exceptional location for observing stars and, occasionally, meteor showers. If you're visiting independently, bring a blanket, warm layers, and binoculars or a telescope to enjoy this magical experience under the stars.

Mount Shasta's Annual 4th of July Fireworks Over Lake Siskiyou

When: July 4th

Location: Lake Siskiyou Camp Resort

The 4th of July fireworks display over Lake Siskiyou is a highlight of the summer season in Mount Shasta. Visitors and locals gather around the lake to watch the fireworks reflect off the water, creating a beautiful, festive scene. This event is family-friendly and draws a large crowd, so arrive early to find a good viewing spot. Many people bring blankets and picnic setups, turning the evening into a lakeside celebration. The fireworks display usually starts shortly after sunset, and the combination of the mountain backdrop and the lake's reflections makes for a truly memorable show.

Holiday Tree Lighting and Caroling

When: December

Location: Downtown Mount Shasta

In December, Mount Shasta's downtown area transforms into a winter wonderland with the annual tree lighting and caroling event. This festive celebration includes carol singing, hot cocoa, and holiday treats, bringing the community together for a cozy night out. The event typically starts in the early evening and culminates with the lighting of the town's Christmas tree. It's a heartwarming way to get into the holiday spirit and enjoy the charm of Mount Shasta's close-knit community.

Safe Night Travel Tips

While Mount Shasta is generally safe, taking a few precautions can help ensure a smooth and enjoyable evening out.

Plan Transportation in Advance

If you're staying outside of downtown or planning to visit nearby areas like Weed, arrange transportation ahead of time. Mount Shasta has limited public transportation, so consider using a designated driver or ride-sharing app if you plan to visit multiple locations or enjoy a few drinks.

Bring Layers for Cooler Evenings

Mount Shasta's mountain climate can result in chilly evenings, even during the warmer months. Bring an extra jacket or sweater if you're planning to be outdoors, especially if you'll be attending events at Bunny Flat or other high-altitude locations. In winter, temperatures can drop significantly, so dressing warmly is essential for comfort.

Stay Aware of Wildlife

It's not uncommon to encounter wildlife near Mount Shasta, especially at night. While encounters are rare, it's best to stay alert, particularly in less populated areas. Drive slowly on rural roads, as deer and other animals can cross unexpectedly. If walking back to your accommodation at night, use a flashlight and stick to well-lit paths.

Stay Hydrated and Snack Smartly

If you're spending the evening exploring bars or music venues, stay hydrated and have a small snack or meal to keep your energy up. Many bars and pubs in Mount Shasta offer light bites and appetizers that pair well with local drinks. Hydration is also important at higher elevations, as it helps prevent altitude sickness.

Summary

Mount Shasta's nightlife may be laid-back, but it offers a variety of options for an enjoyable evening. From sampling local brews at cozy pubs and catching live music to attending seasonal events like fireworks and stargazing, there's something for everyone to enjoy after dark. With a little planning and awareness of safety, you can make the most of Mount Shasta's unique, small-town nightlife and create lasting memories under the stars.

Chapter 21

Appendix

The appendix serves as a quick-reference resource for visitors to Mount Shasta, covering essential contacts, navigational tools, and useful information to enhance your travel experience. From emergency contacts to addresses for popular accommodations and attractions, this section ensures that you have all the necessary details at your fingertips for a safe and organized trip.

A. Emergency Contacts

Having emergency contact information on hand is crucial for any trip. Here are the key numbers to remember while in Mount Shasta:

Emergency Services (Police, Fire, Medical): 911

Mount Shasta Police Department: (530) 926-7540

Mercy Medical Center Mount Shasta: (530) 926-6111

Shasta-Trinity National Forest Ranger Station: (530) 926-4511

Mount Shasta Fire Department: (530) 926-7546

B. Maps and Navigational Tools

Navigating Mount Shasta is easier with a combination of digital and physical maps. Here are a few resources to consider:

Shasta-Trinity National Forest Map: Available at the ranger station or online, this map covers trails, campgrounds, and key points of interest in the national forest.

Google Maps: Most of Mount Shasta's attractions are available on Google Maps, allowing for GPS navigation, real-time updates, and offline maps.

AllTrails: This app is ideal for hikers and offers trail maps, difficulty ratings, elevation profiles, and user reviews for trails in Mount Shasta.

Local Guide Maps: Many local shops and the visitor center offer free maps of the town and surrounding areas, with helpful tips on popular routes and scenic lookouts.

C. Useful Local Phrases

English is the primary language spoken in Mount Shasta, but here are a few handy phrases and expressions that may be useful for visitors:

"Where's the nearest trailhead?" - Useful for finding hiking starting points.

"Is there a parking fee here?" - Helpful for outdoor spots that may require payment.

"Are there any nearby campgrounds?" - Great for locating campsites or camping areas.

"Do you offer vegetarian/vegan options?" - For those with dietary preferences.

"Thank you for sharing this sacred space." - A respectful phrase for use in sacred sites or during spiritual events.

D. Addresses and Locations of Popular Accommodations

Here is a list of popular places to stay in Mount Shasta:

Mount Shasta Resort

Address: 1000 Siskiyou Lake Blvd, Mt Shasta, CA 96067

Phone: (530) 926-3030

Best Western Plus Tree House

Address: 111 Morgan Way, Mt Shasta, CA 96067

Phone: (530) 926-3101

Strawberry Valley Inn

Address: 1142 S Mount Shasta Blvd, Mt Shasta, CA 96067

Phone: (530) 926-2052

Shasta Inn

Address: 1121 S Mount Shasta Blvd, Mt Shasta, CA 96067

Phone: (530) 926-3411

E. Addresses and Locations of Popular Restaurants and Cafes

Enjoy some of the best dining spots in Mount Shasta:

Lily's Restaurant

Address: 1013 S Mount Shasta Blvd, Mt Shasta, CA 96067

Phone: (530) 926-3372

Pipeline Craft Taps & Kitchen

Address: 311 N Mount Shasta Blvd, Mt Shasta, CA 96067

Phone: (530) 918-9234

Seven Suns Coffee & Cafe

Address: 1011 S Mount Shasta Blvd, Mt Shasta, CA 96067

Phone: (530) 926-9701

Black Bear Diner

Address: 401 W Lake St, Mt Shasta, CA 96067

Phone: (530) 926-4669

F. Addresses and Locations of Popular Bars and Clubs

Relax and unwind at these local bars:

Pipeline Craft Taps & Kitchen

Address: 311 N Mount Shasta Blvd, Mt Shasta, CA 96067

The Vet's Club

Address: 406 N Mt Shasta Blvd, Mt Shasta, CA 96067

Mount Shasta Brewing Company

Address: 360 College Ave, Weed, CA 96094

G. Addresses and Locations of Top Attractions

Mount Shasta is filled with natural wonders and scenic spots:

Lake Siskiyou

Address: Lake Siskiyou Camp Resort, 4239 W A Barr Rd, Mt Shasta, CA 96067

Bunny Flat Trailhead

Location: Off Everitt Memorial Highway, approximately 11 miles from downtown Mt Shasta

Panther Meadows

Location: Accessible via Everitt Memorial Highway, near Bunny Flat

Castle Lake

Address: Castle Lake Rd, Mt Shasta, CA 96067

H. Addresses and Locations of Book Shops

For books on Mount Shasta's history, hiking trails, and spiritual significance:

Soul Connections

Address: 321 N Mount Shasta Blvd, Mt Shasta, CA 96067

Phone: (530) 918-9533

Gallery 555 (Books on Local Culture and Art)

Address: 555 N Mount Shasta Blvd, Mt Shasta, CA 96067

Phone: (530) 926-5550

I. Addresses and Locations of Top Clinics, Hospitals, and Pharmacies

For health services and pharmacies:

Mercy Medical Center Mount Shasta

Address: 914 Pine St, Mt Shasta, CA 96067

Phone: (530) 926-6111

Rite Aid Pharmacy

Address: 1036 S Mount Shasta Blvd, Mt Shasta, CA 96067

Phone: (530) 926-3444

Shasta-Trinity National Forest Ranger Station

Address: 204 W Alma St, Mt Shasta, CA 96067

Phone: (530) 926-4511

J. Addresses and Locations of UNESCO World Heritage Sites

Mount Shasta itself is not a UNESCO World Heritage Site; however, nearby locations of significant cultural and ecological value include national parks and conservation areas that honor and protect the unique biodiversity and landscapes of Northern California. Check local guides and websites for more information on nearby protected areas.

Summary

This appendix provides a valuable reference for visitors, covering emergency contacts, maps, addresses, and additional information to enhance travel preparedness and ensure a safe, organized trip. With these details readily available, visitors to Mount Shasta can enjoy peace of mind, allowing them to focus on the beauty, culture, and experiences that make this destination unforgettable.

This completes the Mount Shasta CA Visitor's Guide, with each chapter meticulously crafted to deliver an informative, engaging, and practical resource for all types of travelers. Let me know if there's anything more you'd like to add or adjust!

Map of Mount Shasta

Scan The QR Code With Your Smart Phone To Get The Locations In Real Time

https://maps.app.goo.gl/KJ8WHEGshciecj4R6

Map of Things to do in Mount Shasta

Scan The QR Code With Your Smart Phone To Get The Locations In Real Time

<u>Things to do</u>

Map of Restaurants

Scan The QR Code With Your Smart Phone To Get The Locations In Real Time

Restaurants

Hiking Trails In Mount Shasta

Scan The QR Code With Your Smart Phone To Get The Locations In Real Time

Hiking Trails

Photo/Image Attribution

https://commons.wikimedia.org/wiki/File:MtShasta_aerial.JPG

https://commons.wikimedia.org/wiki/File:Mount_Shasta_as_seen_from_Highway_97-2920.jpg

Made in the USA
Las Vegas, NV
19 December 2024

14746613R00105